THE PAPACY, THE EPISCOPACY, AND COLLEGIALITY

WILHELM BERTRAMS, S.J.

THE PAPACY,

THE EPISCOPACY,
AND
COLLEGIALITY

Translated by Patrick T. Brannan, S.J.

With a Foreword by John J. Reed, S.J.

NP

THE NEWMAN PRESS · WESTMINSTER, MARYLAND · 1964

The present volume is a translation of Latin and Italian studies originally published by the *Pontificia Universita Gregoriana. De relatione inter Episcopatum et Primatum* (Rome, 1963) is an expansion of an earlier study, published in *Periodica de re morali, canonica, liturgica* 51 (1962) under the title, "De relatione inter officium episcopale et primatiale." "De quaestione circa originem potestatis iurisdictionis Episcoporum in Concilio Tridentino non resoluta," originally appeared in *Periodica de re morali, canonica, liturgica* 52 (1963). "La Collegialita Episcopale," was first published in *La Civilta Cattolica* (March, 1964), Quaderno, 2729.

Imprimi potest: JOHN M. DALEY, S.J.
　　　　　　　　Praepositus Provinciae Marylandiae
　　　　　　　　March 4, 1964

Nihil obstat:　　CARROLL E. SATTERFIELD
　　　　　　　　Censor Librorum

Imprimatur:　　LAWRENCE J. SHEHAN, D.D.
　　　　　　　　Archbishop of Baltimore
　　　　　　　　April 24, 1964

Foreword

According to the positive disposition of divine providence the fruits of redemption are to be applied, ordinarily, not in a purely individualistic manner but with dependence upon social cooperation. In the work of redemption God respected, so to speak, the social character implanted in the nature of man in the work of creation. To this end our divine Lord established His Church, as an external, visible, juridically organized society, in which and through the instrumentality of which the human person is to achieve supernatural salvation and sanctification.

The Church, therefore, is a society at the same time supernatural and human. As a supernatural society, its constitution is not framed or changeable by the constituent members but pre-established by God, its founder, and to that extent not discernible by principles of political philosophy but derived from revelation and described in the instruments of the Church's own *magisterium*. But it is also a truly human society, and to that extent it is also subject to the norms and laws of human sociability and organized cooperation. Whoever overlooks or underestimates either of these two elements, the divine and the human, in the constitution of the Church, is predisposed to misunderstand the facts, principles, and processes of her law. In recent times it has often been necessary to stress the Church's divine origin and spiritual character against a tendency to interpret the Church, as society, in terms of natural political science. Today there is some danger of ignoring the reality of her juridic structure.

For many years Father Bertrams has been teaching and writing on principles of what we would call, in our Anglo-American terminology, the constitutional law of the Church. It is one of the most distinctive features of his contributions that he is able to combine so smoothly and to such advantage the two elements of divine institution and human supposition. A second characteristic of Father Bertrams' writing is an extraordinary capacity for synthesis and unification, an ability to perceive a single concept on the basis of which a number of seemingly unrelated facts or principles find their common explanation. By reason of these two qualities, against a background of considerable learning and experience, Father Bertrams is singularly apt for the task which he herein attempts: to define the relationship between the episcopacy and the primacy, so as to answer the great questions, old and new, on the relation of orders and jurisdiction, the dependence of the individual bishop's power upon the papacy in origin and in exercise, the authority of the episcopal college as a whole, the conditions of its actuation, and the harmonizing of its scope with the pre-eminence of the Holy See.

It was often mentioned among the expectations of the Second Vatican Council that, as the First Vatican clarified the status of the pope in terms of infallibility and primacy, the Second should clarify the status of the bishop, not so much in his capacity as pastor and ruler of a particular territory as in his collegial responsibility for the universal Church, and define more precisely his relation to the Roman Pontiff, at issue in both of these aspects of the episcopal office. For this reason Father Bertrams' study comes at a most opportune time (certainly not by mere coincidence) since this is precisely the purpose and burden of his book. Too often such questions are approached on the plane of proximate principles, by juxtaposing and evaluating texts from various documents and arguments from various authorities. Father Bertrams characteristically constructs his synthesis on the basis of a penetrating analysis of the ultimate principles of society in general and of the Church in particular.

It is not the function of a Foreword to anticipate the author's presentation by a preview of his methods or principles of solution. But the reader will be well advised to remember the characteristics which were cited by way of indicating the author's aptitude for this task: his blending of the duality in the social constitution of the Church, and his pursuit of a common theme or principle through disparate applications. This should preclude any temptation to neglect the earlier, more metaphysical portions of the work, under the misapprehension that they might not be significantly related to the whole.

The present volume comes to us, of course, in the form of a translation. The office of the translator is always difficult. He must pick his cautious and conscientious way between two equally obnoxious extremes, the mechanical rendition of equivalent words, on the one hand, and a running paraphrase or commentary, on the other. This is particularly true of the attempt to render into English, or any modern language, a Latin exposition of a legal topic. It is not that the modern language is incapable of expressing law—we do fairly well in our own laws—it is rather that the modern language is incapable of expressing the Latin expression of the law. Father Brannan brings to this problem an intimate familiarity with the classical languages, ample experience in the translation of Latin texts of various species, and an adequate knowledge of the theological and canonical context of the question.

The ultimate result is that this skillful analysis of a timely and vital issue has been made available to the English reader in a translation which effectively presents the author's own ideas and structures of thought, while constituting in its own right an authentic and literary English production.

JOHN J. REED, S.J.

Woodstock College
Woodstock, Maryland

Translator's Preface

The present book is a compilation of several recent studies by Father Wilhelm Bertrams, S.J., Professor of Canon Law at the Gregorian University, Rome. It marks the first appearance of these studies in a single volume and has been so published at the express wish of the author and with the permission of the proprietor of the original articles, the *Pontificia Universita Gregoriana*, Rome. The first article comprises a translation of *De Relatione inter Episcopatum et Primatum* (Rome, 1963) which, as Father Bertrams indicates in his introduction to this volume, is an expansion and development of an earlier study, "De relatione inter officium episcopale et primatiale," which appeared in *Periodica de re morali, canonica, liturgica*, 51 (1962), 3–29. The second article, which is concerned with the Council of Trent, is a translation of the article "De quaestione circa originem potestatis iurisdictionis Episcoporum in Concilio Tridentino non resoluta" from *Periodica de re morali, canonica, liturgica*, 52 (1963), 458–476. The final article, which is properly concerned with the collegiality of the episcopacy, is translated from the original Latin manuscript, provided by Father Bertrams, of an article entitled "La Collegialità Episcopale," *La Civilta Cattolica* (March, 1964) Quaderno 2729, 436–455.

To further the ease with which this volume may be read, I have undertaken to translate the author's citations from their original French, German, Italian, and Latin.

In a few instances (the early Conciliar decrees) I have followed the Greek which, while substantially identical with the Latin, nonetheless gives a clearer sense. All the translations are my own.

Finally, I have the happy, but impossible to fulfill task of expressing my debt and gratitude to several colleagues for their assistance in this project. First and foremost my recognition goes to Father John J. Reed, S.J., Professor of Canon Law at Woodstock College, for technical advice, criticism, and encouragement. The suggestions and clerical assistance of Father Francis F. Burch, S.J., and Father David F. Stokes, S.J., both of Woodstock College, were indispensable and valuable. My translations from the German owe much to the native fluency of Mr. Fritz L. Samson, Librarian at Woodstock College. My text has profited much from these friends, colleagues, and teachers. The limitations of this translation are to be ascribed to the translator alone.

PATRICK T. BRANNAN, S.J.

Woodstock College
Woodstock, Maryland
February, 1964

Contents

THE PAPACY, THE EPISCOPACY, AND COLLEGIALITY

On the Relationship between the Episcopacy and Primacy

Introduction

Our subject in this study is the relationship of the episcopal office to the primatial office. We presuppose what is established from positive sources or contained in existing legislation: "The bishops are the successors of the Apostles and by divine institution are placed in charge of the individual churches which they govern with ordinary power under the authority of the Roman Pontiff" (Can. 329). We presuppose, therefore, that the episcopal office is of divine law and that a bishop has the ordinary power of jurisdiction only through the mediation of the Roman Pontiff. For "whoever is to be consecrated a bishop, even if chosen, presented, or designated by a civil ruler as well, must necessarily have canonical provision or investiture by which he is constituted bishop of a vacant diocese and which can be granted by the Roman Pontiff alone" (Can. 332 § 1).[1]

We realize that the ties between the bishops and the Supreme Pontiff are not merely of the social order; much less are these ties of the merely external social order. Actually, these ties are principally constituted by the charity of Christ our Lord. They are directed toward the building up of the Body of Christ which is the Church (Col. 1:18). They are, of course, sacramentally established and maintained. The sacraments, however, have been entrusted to

1

the Church. As a matter of fact, all of these ties combine to constitute the relationship between the bishops and the Supreme Pontiff. This relationship, however, is necessarily expressed and defined within the Church, as a supernatural but truly human society, by external and juridical notes.

On these suppositions, then, our only concern is this speculative question: What does the episcopal office lack when there is no canonical mission from the Roman Pontiff, as mentioned in Canon 109, or when there is no canonical investiture, as mentioned in Canon 332 § 1? What is the metaphysico-juridical structure of the episcopal office as this office is constituted by divine law and, as thus divinely constituted, is present in a subject? What are the principles of social metaphysics and sacramental-ecclesiological theology which form the basis for the relationship of the episcopal office to the primatial office?

The solution to this question is present in the very structure of human sociability and of human sociability supernaturally elevated in the concrete order of salvation and ordered to a supernatural end. Consequently we are assembling in these pages principles and conclusions which we have already proposed elsewhere on this subject.[2] Since they are of importance for the solution to the question at hand, they shall be briefly explained in the first part of this article. Then, in the second part, these principles and conclusions shall be applied in order to clarify the structure of the episcopal office and its relation to the primatial office.

Notes

1. "The bishops . . . as far as their own dioceses are concerned, as true pastors individually feed and govern the flocks entrusted to them; yet in doing this they are not completely independent but are under the req-

uisite authority of the Roman Pontiff even though they possess ordinary power of jurisdiction immediately communicated to them by the same Supreme Pontiff. Pius XII, Encyclical, *Mystici Corporis Christi,"* Acta Apostolicae Sedis 35 (1943), 211 f. Cf. also the text and commentary edited by Sebastion Tromp, S.J., *Textus et Documenta,* Pont. Univ. Gregorianae, series theologia, 26 (Rome, 1958[3]), § 41, 15, p. 119f.)

2. "De principio subsidiaritatis in iure canonico," *Periodica de re morali, canonica, liturgica,* 46 (1957), 3 ff. "De publicitate iuridica statuum perfectionis Ecclesiae," *ibid.,* 47 (1958), 155 ff. "Die personale Struktur des Kirchenrechts," *Stimmen der Zeit,* 164 (May, 1959), 121 ff. "De personalitatis moralis in iure canonico natura metaphysica," *Periodica de re morali, canonica, liturgica,* 48 (1959), 213 ff. "De effectu consensus matrimonialis naturaliter validi," *Miscellanea in memoriam Petri Cardinalis Gasparri* (Rome: Pontificia Universitas Lateranensis, 1960), pp. 119 ff. "De influxu Ecclesiae in iura baptizatorum," *Periodica de re morali, canonica, liturgica,* 49 (1960), 417 ff. "Das Recht in theologischer Sicht, katholische Auffassungen," *Staatslexikon,* Herausgegeben von der Görres-Gesellschaft, 6 Band (Freiburg i.B., 1961[6]), 621 ff. "De relatione inter officium episcopale et primatiale," *Periodica de re morali, canonica, liturgica,* 51 (1962), 3 ff. "De efficacitate consensus matrimonialis naturaliter validi," *ibid.,* 51 (1962), 288 ff. "Die rechtliche Natur der Zivilehe," *Jahrbuch des Instituts für christliche Sozialwissenschaften* (Münster in Westfalen, 1962), pp. 191 ff.

Part I: *Human Sociability*

1. INTERNAL AND EXTERNAL STRUCTURE OF HUMAN SOCIABILITY
Man—Person

Since man is self-subsistent as well as self-possessed in virtue of an intentional control over his acts, man is a person, i.e., a spiritual nature that comprises an ontological and intentional entirety. The person is supreme in terms of being and good. For a spiritual nature is ordered to all truth and goodness, and is consequently directly ordered to infinite truth and goodness, that is, to God Himself. This ordination to infinite truth and goodness, however, is realized through an infinite number of acts since a finite spiritual nature is in potency to infinite truth and goodness and is virtually their embodiment. Human nature, however, as a spiritual nature substantially united to a body, achieves its proper perfection in space and time. That is to say, by gradual change, by having a history, it transcends itself and acquires the objective goodness contained in the universe for itself.[1] It must be observed, therefore, that human values in the proper sense have an intentional being. This being is interior to man and ontologically inheres in his soul as an accidental reality. Consequently, human values afford man a perfection proper to himself, i.e., a personal perfection.

4

The realization of the individual's personality gives rise to social relations, and the basis of human sociability is the personality of man. Consequently, human nature is essentially social. Because man is composed of body and soul which are essential constitutive parts, human sociability is with metaphysical necessity made up of an internal and an external element which are its essential parts.

The internal structure of human sociability[2] is determined by common human values since the realization of these values is the internal end of social life. For the center of social life is and always will be man as a person, as an agent subject. Man strives for personal perfection in the midst of other coexistent men. Men are mutually related since they owe one another reciprocal recognition, respect, and good will as persons, and since all these communications may be made conducive to the acquisition of personal perfection.[3] The means for such reciprocal, personal communications are—as long as the person itself is incommunicable—the human good in its unlimited extension, i.e., all those goods contained in the concept "humanity," or those values which afford man his personal perfection, namely, the values of culture, civilization, economy, etc. Accordingly one's own perfection as a person, as well as the perfection of others, is reached by reciprocal intentionality, and the realization of human values produces an internal, i.e., intentional, coordination of persons[4] which is the formal constitutive element of human sociability. The internal structure of human sociability is constituted by the intentional ordering of persons to the various human, common (to persons) values since these common human values form a unit because they are ordered to the development of personality. These human values are truly common since they are realized by means of metaphysical

5

solidarity, namely, by the common intentional union of all.

Personal freedom in the realization of human values is included within this internal coordination of persons. That is to say, man has the moral faculty to realize human values.[5] Therefore, since the common human values are the object of such a moral faculty and of all the intentional relationships among coexistent men, they make up the internal structure of social life.

Furthermore, this internal structure of sociability must be realized in external social life. For men are not capable of merely internal communication. Man is composed of body and soul which are substantially united. Through his body man is placed in time and space. Specifically human activity is, consequently, spiritual, intentional activity that is externally expressed and manifested in and through the body, and thus exercises a causality that is in the full sense human.[6] This external element is, therefore, an essential element which is metaphysically necessary for the constitution of human sociability and for its efficacy in space and time, i.e., among coexistent men.

Consequently, an external order or organization is required for the external expression and manifestation of intentional relationships among men. For without this order social relationships could not serve their purpose. The external structure of social life is present, therefore, in such an external order or organization.[7] The *external structure* of sociability is the external transposition of the internal structure; in the external structure the internal structure is transposed to the exterior; the internal structure determines the external structure. Consequently the external structure cannot determine, disregard, or change the internal structure; for "this would *per impossibile* mean that

6

the mode of organizing would as such determine what is already by its very concept antecedent as the thing to be organized, namely, the internal structure of social life with its objective 'common values' (the person with its cultural and religious values)."[8]

Fundamental Rights and Juridical Institutions

The moral faculty of realizing human values, inasmuch as this is a faculty of external activity, a faculty ordained to operation in social life, establishes man's *fundamental rights.*[9] These rights are, of course, principally possessed in regard to the inviolability of the person itself, inasmuch as human life, corporeal integrity, and freedom of conscience are related to the very substance of man, a spiritual-corporeal being, who, as such, has an absolute value because of his divine destiny and who is not a means to the end of others. Thus man situated in the social life is protected. He is protected in his very person to the perfection of which all human values are referred and which would be illusory without such protection of the person.

Furthermore man's fundamental rights are constituted by freedom in the attainment of the various human values external to man. Man is the subject of rights in the realization of human values. Indeed the faculties of activity, which form the substance (namely the spiritual, intentional, internal-to-man being) of fundamental rights, constitute the dynamic aspects of the personality itself, i.e., the personality considered under the aspect of activity inasmuch as the person is endowed with liberty in his activity towards his end. Such faculties of activity specify personal liberty with respect to its objects: human goods ordered to man and to be obtained by man who is by essence social, by

7

man placed among coexistent men. Accordingly, fundamental rights as well as the human values to be realized constitute the internal structure of human sociability in its substance; for these rights are referred to these goods and these goods are the object of these rights. These rights are something personal; they partake of the absolute value of the person.[10]

Those rights which are numbered among the fundamental rights (e.g., the right to acquire material goods as one's own, the right to contract marriage, the right to work, etc.) are expressly limited by objective principles. Such principles explain a particular right in terms of the nature of the object, i.e., in terms of the specific nature of the value to be realized, e.g., matrimony. Thus these principles form an ideal objective whole which is stably present antecedent to, and independent of, the human will which realizes such a human value in the concrete. For this reason this ideal whole is spoken of as a juridical *institution*: because fundamental rights are exercised in realized sociability, in external social life.

For the same reason such institutions need principles which are necessary consequences of the exercise of rights by coexistent men. Indeed, the exercise of fundamental rights cannot be accomplished in an orderly manner unless account is taken of the mutual dependence and interdependence by which coexistent men are reciprocally related in every phase of the realization of human values. Hence principles concerning the coordination of the exercise of rights in all its phases arise from the very nature of the subject, i.e., from the exercise of these rights. The complex of all these principles objectively constitutes the external structure of human sociability, inasmuch as the common good (in the technical sense)[11] is objectively determined

8

in order that it may be able to be actually realized.

It is clear from the above that these objective principles (of both species) are concerned with an obligatory norm for social activity, or constitute a true, objective, natural right. These principles, therefore, have their foundation in the human person itself and its absolute value; consequently, these principles are present antecedent to and independent of every organized association, both concrete and abstract. Indeed, considered in their ultimate formality, the provisions of these principles are reduced to the divine essence and their binding force imposed by the divine will.[12]

Organized Association

There can be no efficacious coordination of the exercise of rights in every phase of the realization of human values without associations by which this coordination is accomplished. There is no call in this context for further explanation of the elements relating to such associations. Suffice it to note that the coordination of the exercise of rights in its totality belongs to the State, and that the State's internal end is the establishment and conservation of order and peace in society by the fact that the exercise of rights is totally coordinated. Under these circumstances fundamental rights can be efficaciously and peacefully exercised. Consequently, *the State* is rightly called an organized association, because organization is a true human value just as the body itself constitutes a true value for man. Hence intentional bonds can be had between men through organizational values. Indeed, among organized associations the State is utterly necessary.

And this is due to the fact that the objective principles of natural law, which define the common good, are not

9

fully determined in every case. Moreover, the concrete social life is in a state of perpetual evolution and change. Hence the requirements for the maintenance of social order and peace vary with different circumstances of time, place, culture, technology, etc. Accordingly, there is an ever new need for concrete determination of the principles of natural law and their application to actual circumstances by positive law. Finally a principle is demanded which will so direct everyone that they efficaciously cooperate towards the realization of the common good. These details, therefore, are the concern of civil authority. It follows then that civil authority has the subjective right so to order and coordinate everything in the state that the common good may be realized.[13] This subjective right, therefore, is of the public order; it includes public legislative, executive and juridical power. In other respects the internal and external structures of this right are to be explained exactly as we did in the case of man's fundamental rights.[14]

As far as the legislative power in particular is concerned, to maintain the common good the State creates *positive law* which orders the exercise of rights through the concrete determination of the principles of natural law and through their application to actual circumstances.[15]

The coordinating function of public authority is not, therefore, concerned with man's fundamental rights themselves and their exercise as such.[16] For these rights constitute personality in action; the person is antecedent to every organized society. Organization is for the benefit of the person. Public authority can, however, exert an influence on the exercise of fundamental rights to maintain the common good of society. For this is the end for which it is constituted. Moreover, the effects of the exercise of fundamental rights exert an influence on society. Consequently, because of such effects organized society can exert influence on the exercise of rights.

The Constitution of Rights through Juridical Activity

Man exercises his fundamental rights by a particular act that is ordained to the attainment of human good, and which, therefore, is also constituted by an internal and external element. Actually, a *juridical act* or juridical transaction is an act of the will which is externally manifested in order to possess the juridical effect intended. When such an act is placed in accordance with its essential constitutive elements, the mere act exercises its causality and a concrete (acquired) right is established. Thus, e.g., through a bill of sale ownership of the thing purchased is acquired. Organized society exercises its influence in this transaction when for the common good it restricts the exercise of fundamental rights or demands a definite procedure. The exercise of rights without the observance of such regulations is not recognized as lawful, and perhaps is even forbidden. In such cases the effects proper to a lawful exercise of rights are not had.

Consequently, a distinction must be made between the *existence* of, and the *efficacy* of juridical acts.[17] An act exists if all its essential constitutive elements, the internal and external elements, are present. If an essential element is lacking, the act is non-existent. An act is juridically efficacious if it is not only existent but also if the requisite external structure is also present. Indeed, the external structure is an essential element of the act. Nonetheless, for the sake of the common good the requisite external structure—namely, the constitution of an act in a determined way in social life—can be impeded by civil authority by the

11

placing of an obstacle (extrinsic, of course, to the act as such). As long as such an obstacle remains, the existent juridical act is not coordinated with the exercise of the rights of others because it is against the common good. The existent act lacks requisite incorporation within social life and, hence, the requisite external structure: it simply lacks the external structure. Therefore the act is juridically inefficacious.

Accordingly, in this case (of a certainly existing but inefficacious juridical act) the right to be constituted by the juridical act lacks an essential element. Because of the lack of coordination with the rights of others the act itself lacks its proper external structure; hence, such a right is not completely constituted. The right is indeed constituted in its internal element or substantially, namely, in its intentional being which inheres in the soul as an accident. But such a right lacks its requisite external structure, i.e., one adapted to a particular society. In other words, it simply lacks its "body," and because of this defect the right is not efficacious. If, for example, transferral of ownership of property must be effected before a notary, the concrete right to the property is constituted substantially, i.e., in its intentional being by a manifested act of the will, but it has no efficacy without a notary.

It is certainly true that the external structure is not an extrinsic accretion to the right. For, of itself, this consists in the transposition of the right's internal structure to the outside. The right itself is constituted a complete whole with its internal and external structures by the (manifested) activity of the subject's will. The right's external structure, as such, is constituted together with the right that is constituted in its intentional being, precisely because the internal structure of itself transposes itself to the outside. It aims at this objective: the possession of its own "body" in order to have efficacy. In this sense it is commonly said that an acquired right is efficaciously constituted by an agent subject, provided that the norms of natural law are observed. These norms are taken to mean the ones which are determined by the nature of the value in question, e.g., ownership of property (proprietorship).

It is, however, the function of public authority to coordinate the exercise of the rights of coexistent men. Hence, it is the function of public authority to coordinate the exercise of rights in its totality, or in the light of the mutual interdependence of men living together in a concrete society. This is why public authority, through the imposition of a determined procedure for the efficacious exercise of rights, places an obstacle that is extrinsic to the activity of the will, in order that the external structure of a right, which is constituted in its intentional being by the agent subject, may not be constituted unless such a prescribed procedure is followed. In such a case the act of the subject exercises its causality with respect to the substance or intentional being of the right to be constituted. But the act's causality is impeded with respect to the requisite external structure of the right to be constituted, or, in other words, the right cannot be efficaciously constituted.

In brief, a juridical act, existing in its essential constitutive elements, constitutes a right *in its substance* and internal structure, in its intentional being. Such an act when it is not placed in accordance with the legitimate determinations of public authority cannot efficaciously constitute a right. For the causality of the act is *juridically* impeded in its requisite external structure and, consequently, in its *efficacious* being. In other words such a right is simply not yet had. If the prescribed procedure is followed, the causal-

13

ity of the act immediately extends to the external structure as well. The right is also efficaciously or completely constituted. Accordingly, the right itself is constituted by the juridical act of the agent subject, not by recognition on the part of public authority.[18] Public authority "grants recognition" to something which was constituted as a complete whole by the agent subject as an efficient cause.

2. THE INTERNAL AND EXTERNAL STRUCTURE OF SUPERNATURALLY ELEVATED HUMAN SOCIABILITY AND OF THE CHURCH
Personality and the Fundamental Rights of the Supernatural Order

In the concrete order of salvation a supernatural end has been set for man. The order in question is the supernatural order, i.e., the order proper to (the Triune) God insofar as he "dwells in light inaccessible" (1 Tim. 6:16) and as such is to be gained or possessed in the beatific vision. The author and head of this concrete order of salvation is *Christ the Lord*. Supernatural revelation—the truths to be believed and the norms to be followed—is definitively perfected and completed in and through Him. The new life, which truly inaugurates the vision of God, is acquired for men by His passion and death especially. Indeed, this life is had by participation in Christ's life: "But Christ lives in me" (Gal. 2:20).

Therefore, man's intentionality is not only increased as far as its object is concerned, but also is elevated to an essentially higher order, to the supernatural. For man is allowed to live a supernatural life efficaciously and fruitfully. Yet all of these effects are had only if man is united with Christ. Baptism is especially necessary for such union

14

with Christ as this is objectively required in the present order of salvation: "Amen, amen I say to thee, unless a man be born again of water, and the Holy Spirit, he cannot enter into the kingdom of God" (John 3:5).

By baptism, therefore, man's personality is supernaturally elevated so that by his own supernaturally elevated activity he can efficaciously and fruitfully live a supernatural life. In this sense the personality of the supernatural order is constituted by baptism. For, while man by his very nature enjoys a personality of the natural order, he does not by his very nature enjoy the requisite personality with reference to his supernatural end. We are here concerned only with that human condition which in the present state of salvation man ought to have objectively, ordinarily, and consequent to the divine will by which this supernatural order is constituted. We are not treating of the subjective salvation of individual men, nor are we investigating how even the unbaptized can attain a supernatural end, notwithstanding the principle—cited above—enunciated by the Lord Himself about the necessity of baptism for the attainment of the kingdom of God. For such questions have no bearing upon the question that is presently the sole object of our consideration, namely, the ordinary structure of human sociability as objectively intended according to God's will. The supernatural order is the order of salvation established by Christ the Lord on the Cross and is, for this reason, proper to Him as its Head. Hence a capacity to act in this supernatural order can be had only because man is morally united with Christ. The action which effects this requisite union with Christ is baptism. For by baptism, insofar as its reception is a personal action, man manifests his intention of uniting himself as much as he can with Christ offering Himself to His Father on the Cross. Furthermore, Christ the Lord is the principal agent in the conferral of baptism since the sacraments are vicarious actions of Christ.[19]

Thus the principal effect of baptism is the *impression of the baptismal character* by which the baptized person is morally united with and incorporated into Christ, is configured to Christ and marked as bound to Him. Man is not merely extrinsically ordered to Christ, but is ontologically and intrinsically consecrated to Him inasmuch as the baptismal character is a supernatural quality that inheres in the soul as an intentional being. By the baptismal character man is made capable of receiving the supernatural life and, once it is received, of developing and perfecting it, thereby properly, efficaciously and fruitfully striving for his supernatural personal end. Hence man's personality is by no means taken away by baptism because supernatural elevation accidentally affects man's being. Man remains a supposit or a substance, as a whole subsisting in himself. On the contrary, by baptism his personality is intrinsically elevated to the supernatural order. In other words, his metaphysical totality, which is human nature, achieves its proper perfection only in that order which terminates in the beatific vision of God. The baptismal character makes man capable of properly and efficaciously striving for this end— the only end for man in the concrete order of salvation. Intentional control over his acts, which is proper to man, is now possessed with reference to this end. The realization of the spirituality of human nature is increased as greatly as possible since man is elevated to a qualitatively superior order, to an order proper to the Triune God. Hence man's very personality is qualitatively elevated and increased. The baptized person has a supernatural end, the possession of

16

God in the beatific vision, as his personal end which is to be efficaciously and properly attained through personal activity. Indeed, baptism confers the specific freedom of striving for a supernatural end, insofar as it frees man from the law of fallen nature, from the obstacles that hinder his pursuit of his supernatural end (Gal. 4:26; 5:1; 5:13; 5:21; Rom. 8:21).

For it is already clear from the fact that a man is obliged to receive baptism from another, i.e., by a social act, that the supernatural life is to be possessed socially. Actually, Christ the Lord so established the supernatural order that the supernatural life ordinarily must be socially possessed and perfected. Through the reception of baptism man's personality is not only internally elevated, but in the social life as well the baptized individual is set up as a person with respect to the attainments of a supernatural end. For his internally, supernaturally elevated personality is also juridically extended to the supernatural order since the baptized person properly becomes *the subject of rights and duties* with respect to the realization of a supernatural good.

The exercise of activity relative to the acquisition of the supernatural end is specified by this end (acts of faith, worship, charity, the moral virtues, etc.). Therefore, the end to be attained by the baptized enjoins duties that correspond to his supernatural elevation. Thus his freedom is linked up with this end, and the end, furthermore, specifies the means that are necessary to acquire it. In other respects, however, the selection of means to attain the end is left to the freedom of the baptized. For the baptized would not enjoy personal freedom in the exercise of activity relative to the attainment of the supernatural end, unless there were a sphere of external activity in which there is

17

the inviolable faculty to act freely in regard to certain concrete objects: e.g., freedom of conscience, of choice of one's state of life (matrimony, virginity), freedom in communication and associating with the rest of the faithful or in the exercise of charity, etc. Personal freedom relative to personal, supernatural perfection is determined by such faculties in the baptized. Accordingly, these capacities to act are constituted by the supernatural personality itself in its dynamic aspects.

While the fundamental rights of the person of the natural order are derived from his capacities for free activity, his natural powers do not of themselves suffice for the pursuit of a supernatural end. Therefore, additional faculties of exacting the requisite specific means necessary for the acquisition of the supernatural end must be had. For, on the one hand, natural powers do not suffice for the pursuit of the supernatural end which must be necessarily obtained, and on the other, Christ the Lord has instituted such specific means (e.g., the sacraments). All such faculties of acting and exacting, substantially and ontologically, constitute an intentional being, as long as it inheres in the soul through the baptismal character. Because such faculties are possessed to be exercised in social life, they truly constitute *the fundamental rights of the baptized in the supernatural order*. And these rights are ordered to the realization of the supernatural good through the personal activity of the baptized who are united for this purpose.

Actually, the assumption of human nature by the person of the Word, the Son of God, consecrated human nature in the totality of its faculties. Hence all of social life must also be filled and informed with the life of Christ that it be capable of representing the fullness of Christ. Man's very sociability has been supernaturally ele-

18

vated and, as such, must be brought to perfection.[20] Insofar as the *fullness of Christ* must be realized by the cooperation of all, the supernatural good must be realized. Therefore the continuous human realization of the supernatural good constitutes one of the common human values[21] and the object of the intentional relationships of the baptized. For these relationships are ordered to the actuation of this good.

The supernatural good, as possessed by man, includes in its entirety many particular values (the value of faith, worship, charity, etc.)—we are prescinding from the fact that men can realize the fullness of Christ only in a limited way by finite acts—and there are intentional relationships referring to the possession of these values. As a whole, therefore, these relationships are ordained to the realization of the fullness of Christ among men, to the development and completion of the supernatural personal perfection of the baptized. Therefore such relationships constitute supernaturally elevated human sociability.

The baptized are united to one another by supernaturally elevated human intentionality because they are united with, through, and in Christ. Hence they are united in the supernatural good which the Lord Himself has established and which they must actuate by means of an indefinite number of particular supernatural values. Consequently, these particular values are what constitute the internal structure of supernaturally elevated human sociability. In this way human life as a whole is consecrated because the fullness of Christ is realized: "All things have been created through and unto him; and he is before all creatures and in him all things hold together" (Col. 1:16–17). Therefore, it is necessary "to re-establish all things in Christ" (Eph. 1:10).

The Supernatural Good Is Entrusted to the Church

The Church was founded by Christ the Lord to perform the function of realizing the fullness of Christ. For the Church as a supernatural society could not be the product of man's social powers as such. Yet the Church, consequent to her establishment by Christ the Lord, developed as a truly human society.[22] Of course all of the baptized have the common obligation of realizing the supernatural good —through acts of worship of God, through the profession of faith, through works of charity, etc.; in brief, through a life which has been informed with the supernatural spirit. But because of this duty a special function is incumbent upon the Church, and certainly upon the Church's clerics.[23]

For although all the faithful, both as individuals and as a community, have the duty of realizing the supernatural good, nevertheless, to accomplish this, special cooperation is also required on the part of the Church's clerics. The function in question is one which is completely proper to the Church and which, for example, the State does not have. The State is under no personal obligation to realize common human goods. This is rather the duty of individual men and their freely established associations. But natural powers are of themselves ineffectual with respect to the supernatural end. Hence it is the Church's office to confer upon men through a power utterly proper to herself those supernatural means which they need to be able to realize the fullness of Christ and, consequently, to pursue the supernatural end.

Moreover, this substantially supernatural good, namely, the supernatural life in itself, is a quality which inheres in the soul as an intentional being. Hence it is something purely spiritual and internal to man which, as such, cannot

20

be subject to the Church, considered as a human society. Actually the supernatural good is entrusted to the Church because this good is had in a human way, i.e., by external acts (which have been given a spiritual, supernatural efficacy by God).[24] The Church has been entrusted with the value of worship, which she renders to God especially through the Eucharistic sacrifice; with the value of the sanctification of men, especially through the sacraments; with the deposit of doctrine transmitted by Christ which contains the truths to be believed and the norms (precepts and counsels) to be followed. There must be a constant renewal of the value of worship and of sanctification, and this in the way which was substantially established by Christ the Lord. Consequently, it is for this purpose that the power of orders or the sacerdotal order is had in the Church.[25] Christ the Lord transmitted the deposit of doctrine to the Church that she might keep it undiminished as well as propose it to, and impose it upon, men. In such cases no new decisions are made as far as the doctrine transmitted by Christ is concerned. For this doctrine was already completely constituted. But still, the truths and norms must constantly receive new application to all the latest related questions. To perform this task, the power of jurisdiction consisting of the magisterium and government is had in the Church.[26] The directives of the power of jurisdiction are aimed at ordering the activity of the faithful to the supernatural end, through acts of the theological and moral virtues.

It is clear, then, that the supernatural good which must be humanly possessed determines the internal end and *the internal structure* of the Church, of her social activity as a society which is certainly supernatural but also truly human. Consequently, the specific activity of the Church's clerics is necessary for the realization of the supernatural good. For this is the purpose of the power that they possess in regard to worship and sanctification as well as to preaching and applying the doctrine transmitted by Christ.

Moreover the possession of the fundamental rights of the supernatural order (Can. 87) is connected with the reception of these supernatural values from the Church (Can. 682): participation in worship, instruction in the truths transmitted by Christ, direction in Christian living.

The power of the Church corresponds to these rights since the sacred power that is related to the conferral of these supernatural values upon the faithful constitutes the moral faculty of operation of the Church's clerics, a faculty constituted by Christ Himself. Really, the fundamental rights of the supernatural order and the powers of clerics are had through baptism and the sacrament of orders respectively[27]—all sacraments are vicarious actions of Christ. The rights of the baptized inhere in the baptismal character which unites the baptized with Christ; the sacred power inheres in the character of orders by which the ordained shares Christ's priesthood in a specific way.[28] These rights and this power constitute in substance and existence a quality or intentional being which inheres in the soul through the sacramental character. Since they are ordered to the realization of the supernatural good or to the development of the fullness of Christ in men, these rights and this power constitute the internal structure of supernaturally elevated human sociability, a structure which the Lord Christ Himself sacramentally established. Accordingly, since Christ is antecedent to the Church as a human society, the internal structure of supernaturally elevated human sociability is also antecedent to the Church as a human society and cannot be touched by it. Just as the internal structure of human sociability is internal to persons, so also the internal structure of supernaturally elevated human sociability constitutes a personal quality, namely, an intentional being internal to persons.

The Church: an Organized Association

Nevertheless, the internal structure of human sociability, even as elevated to the supernatural, cannot lack organization and external order. Hence, those statements which we made about the metaphysical necessity of the need for external structure in the social life must also be applied to the Church.

The Church was constituted by Christ the Lord as an organized association.[29] The Church has another function besides that directly ordered to the supernatural good: it is the Church's duty to create an objective social order in which social peace is enjoyed so that the faithful can efficaciously pursue their supernatural end. Actually, this is the reason why it is the function of the Church to order the exercise of the faithful's fundamental rights of both the natural and the supernatural order; for all human activity is to be ordered to a supernatural end. Hence, it is the Church's function to organize social life in terms of the supernatural end that is to be attained. An intentional union of the faithful is present even in this organizational type of value by which the Church is made a social totality.[30]

There is no call for further explanation of these points in the present context. The only thing to be noted is that the affirmation that the internal end of the Church is also to order the exercise of the faithful in all its phases, is not an affirmation of the direct authority of the Church in temporal affairs. The organizational authority of the

Church is directed to a supernatural end; the Church comes into contact with temporal affairs only because of the supernatural end. Consequently the competence of societies of the natural order is not affected. Indeed, in general, no directions affect that activity itself in temporal affairs. Rather, the magisterium of the Church through its doctrinal principles instructs the faithful on the morality of engaging in an activity.

Since the very nature of the external structure of sociability consists in a formation or transposition to the outside of an internal structure, all the activity of the Church, even organizational, is ordained to supernatural good. Indeed, the activity of the Church, in preaching God's word and imposing Christ's truths and precepts, is an organizational type of activity. For the truths themselves are already present because they were passed on by Christ the Lord. The Church "disperses," i.e., proposes, imposes, and authoritatively applies them to actual circumstances by doctrinal decrees, precepts and prohibitions.[31] As a consequence of this strict connection between the external and internal structure of the Church, the Church's very organization, its very common good is, as a matter of fact, of a supernatural character, although the nature of its activity is not as a consequence changed.[32] All the social activity of the Church has, consequently, a supernatural character.

The Supernatural Good Is Institutionally Entrusted to the Church

Hence it is clear that the double function of the Church's social activity—the realization of the supernatural good that is to be possessed in a human way and the organization of activity toward possession of the supernatural good in a human way—although formally distinct, is in concrete social activity as closely connected as possible. For the supernatural good is to be actuated by human social activity. Therefore, some organization is always required even in the case of an activity which directly produces (ex opere operato) supernatural life in itself, such as in the Eucharistic sacrifice and the sacraments.[33] In this sense the organizational function encompasses all of the Church's activity.[34] Accordingly, it should be remarked that, consequent to the establishment of the Church as a supernatural but human society by Christ the Lord and consequent to the conferral of a related authority, the supernatural good is institutionally or juridically present in the Church by the will of Christ the Lord. Actually the supernatural good is had in the total complexus of the Church's juridical institutions. Just as the Incarnation of the Word is justly, although analogously, called the primordial sacrament because through the human nature and activity of Christ the Lord the supernatural life is conferred upon men, so also the Church, an external institutional society, as the continued Incarnation of the Word, is justly called the primordial sacrament, or the visible sign instituted by Christ, objectively i.e., ex opere operantis Ecclesiae, efficacious of grace. All the external activity of the Church indicates and reveals her internal, invisible, spiritual, and supernatural life and effects, preserves, increases, and perfects this supernatural life in an institutional manner.[35]

The supernatural human good, therefore, in all of its phases has been institutionally entrusted to the Church by Christ the Lord. Consequently, the social activity of the Church, its juridical activity, has an effect which it could not have of itself, an effect which it owes rather to the activity of Christ, Who manages through the Church an institutional society. It is, therefore, true that the Church's social activity, as human activity, does not of itself have any relation to the supernatural good in itself. This activity is raised to the supernatural order by the fact that the Holy Spirit intrinsically informs the Church's social activity so that it becomes suited to effect the supernatural good in itself. This is why the Church is the body of Christ: because the Holy Spirit as the Spirit of Christ (Rom. 8:9; Gal. 4:6) penetrates the Church as its soul; hence, its life should truly be considered as the life of Christ. The Church's activity is, therefore, human or social activity. But this external activity is not self-subsistent; it does not have an end in itself. This activity proceeds from the internal, invisible life of the Church, from the life of Christ which the Holy Spirit, the soul of the Body of Christ, communicates to the Church. And at the same time this internal life is the end of the Church's external activity, to which its elements are completely ordained.[36]

Accordingly, under the influence of the Holy Spirit the social and juridical activity of the Church is elevated to the supernatural order and thus has supernatural effects which it would be incapable of having of itself. In this sense this same Holy Spirit truly "bound" Himself to the institutional activity of the Church, which owes to this "binding" the fact that it is never null or void. Christ the Lord did not make His Church a charismatic society which would be without "institutions," i.e., juridical norms, juridical duties, and their inherent authority, because in the merely charismatic society there could be no talk of a supernatural good to be possessed in a human or institutional way; and in such a society the supernatural good would not be an objectively certain reality.

26

The supernatural good in the Church truly constitutes an objectively certain reality since it is had through institutions in a juridical way. Thus man, through the valid reception of baptism, is signed with a character which refers him to Christ and which thus binds him to the Body of Christ, which is the Church. This character is a reality. namely, an intentional being, inhering in the soul of the baptized. Although it is invisible in itself, since it is spiritual, it is nonetheless visible—hence, a true sign—in its cause, i.e., in the proper conferral and reception of baptism, which is an external act, a juridical institution, and a juridical transaction. This is why a man becomes a person in the Church through baptism (Can. 87): because the baptized individual is internally referred to Christ, to the Body of Christ, to the Church, he is also the subject of rights and duties in the Church as an external and juridical society.

We have already stated that the faculties of acting and exacting with respect to the acquisition of the personal supernatural end are destined to be exercised in social life, i.e., in association with the rest of the faithful. For this reason they are transposed—at least supposing what will be treated below—to the outside and form an external structure without which they cannot be socially efficacious, but through which they are efficaciously located within the social life of the Church.

Similarly, as a result of a duly performed ordination, objective certitude is had that the power of Christ has been conferred upon a subject (a cleric) and inheres in his soul as an intentional being through the character of orders. The subject of such power can, through juridical transactions, realize the supernatural good whose reality is objectively certain, namely, in the power properly bestowed and repeatedly exercised, or in a juridical institution and juridical activity, e.g., in the administration of the sacraments.

Accordingly, the supernatural good that has been institutionally entrusted to the Church which must be realized by juridical activity has as its subject both the baptized and the ordained and must be realized by their *personal activity*.

The Influence of the Church upon the Juridical Activity of the Baptized

Since the Church is an organized association and a juridical society, she has been entrusted with the administration of all the means of salvation in this concrete supernatural order of salvation. It is, therefore, the Church's function to coordinate the exercise of the fundamental rights of the baptized on the supernatural order and furthermore, indeed, on the natural order *because of the supernatural end* which must be attained.[37]

The Church's social juridical power of affecting the juridical activity of the baptized is not concerned with their fundamental rights, either on the natural or supernatural order.[38] For the former are based directly upon the metaphysical personality of man, the latter upon the sacramental character conferred through baptism, which is the vicarious action of Christ. Consequently, by reason of their substance, in other words, by reason of the moral faculties of acting and demanding on the intentional order, these rights constitute the internal structure of human sociability, be it a natural or supernaturally elevated one. It is the Church's function to coordinate the exercise of fundamental rights; hence, its power is concerned with the external structure of *human sociability*.

Consequently, the Church cannot affect the existence of juridical acts which the baptized properly performed, but she can affect the juridical efficacy of these acts. A good illustration of this matter is found in matrimony (*in fieri*), which is not only a juridical act but also a sacrament (between the baptized).

Matrimony is the result of the properly manifested consent of the parties. Such consent (matrimony *in fieri*) is the sole and adequate cause of matrimony *in facto esse* according to its internal and external structure. Organized society (the State for unbaptized parties, the Church for the baptized) can justly demand for the common good that the matrimonial consent be given in a determined way. Thus the Church demands *canonical form* for Catholics. Even though canonical form has not been observed, the properly given and manifested consent of the parties still exists. Accordingly, such consent constitutes matrimony in its substance or in its intentional being. Nevertheless, such consent cannot exercise its full causality because an external obstacle is placed to prevent the potentiality of the consent from passing into act in regard to the external structure of matrimony. The constitution of this marriage is not, therefore, coordinated with the rights of the rest of the faithful; it is not incorporated within the Church. Hence the requisite external structure cannot arise. In this sense matrimony is not completely constituted by consent that lacks canonical form and is simply not valid. For it lacks an essential element, namely, external structure, and consequently, juridical efficacy.

Therefore the *intentional being of matrimony* is constituted, and its internal structure is had by means of properly given and manifested consent (existent consent). (The internal structure of marriage is the immediate consequence of its ordination toward the values of marriage; hence, the rights and obligations proper to matrimony are contained within it.) Matrimony, therefore, is had in its intentional being through a properly given and manifested consent even though this consent lacks canonical form. The external structure required in the Church is lacking in such a marriage. Hence an essential element is lacking, and because of this lack the marriage is rendered *juridically inefficacious*; the very matrimonial rights themselves are not efficaciously constituted. The marriage is simply invalid. But since the external structure of matrimony is constituted by the transportation of the internal structure to the outside, then certainly nothing further is required to establish this external structure than the removal of the obstacle placed by the Church.

Therefore, the Church can, if it wishes to do so, recognize a substantially constituted marriage which suffers from a defect of canonical form and is, consequently, inefficacious and invalid. Such a recognition takes place through a *sanatio in radice*. That the marriage may become simply valid, i.e., that it may become juridically efficacious or attain its natural juridical efficacy, new activity on the part of the spouses is not of itself required. Rather, when the Church removes the obstacles by waiving canonical form for this particular marriage, the marriage, already existing in its intentional being, immediately acquires its efficacy. For the matrimonial consent, which was properly given and still persists, fully exercises its causality and extends it to the external structure of marriage. From this moment the marriage is simply valid; the matrimonial bond becomes juridically effective; the matrimonial rights possess efficacy and can, therefore, be exercised.[39]

It should be noted that a marriage which is invalid

because of a defect of canonical form cannot be a *sacrament*. Christ the Lord raised the efficacious matrimonial contract to the dignity of a sacrament. To have a sacrament, therefore, existent consent is not sufficient; there must also be efficacious consent. Accordingly, the Church by preventing the efficacy of consent prevents the sacrament also.

In general, therefore, it must be said that the Church can establish an *essential condition* for the recognition of a juridical act.[40] When this essential condition has not been fulfilled, the juridical act lacks the internal structure legally required by the Church in virtue of the common good. The causality of an act that is otherwise properly performed does indeed substantially, i.e., in its substance and internal structure, constitute the right which must be juridically constituted. The condition imposed by the Church is certainly extrinsic to the act as such, since it is imposed through an externally manifested will. Nevertheless, the obstacle is so placed from the outside that the causality of the act cannot pass to the production of the external structure of the right to be constituted. When the right to be constituted has no external structure, this right is not completely constituted because it lacks an essential element. This right is inefficacious; it is not validly constituted.

A similar explanation holds for the influence that the Church exercises over the juridical transactions which aim at supernatural value. Thus, for example, the fundamental rights of the baptized on the supernatural order are constituted by the valid reception of baptism. The moral faculty of acting or exacting, which constitutes the substance of these rights, is based upon the baptismal character. It is, therefore, conferred by every valid reception of baptism. (By the substance of a right is understood its very inten-

31

tional being which is rooted in the sacramental character insofar as it is ordered to the realization and possession of various supernatural values.) Nevertheless, the reception of baptism (though validly received), if it is not accompanied by *the profession of faith and union with the Church,* is not recognized by the Church in the sense that through such baptism the supernatural goods can be neither realized nor sought in the Church. Consequently, baptism without the profession of faith and union with the Church has no juridical effects in the Church.[41]

Baptism, even in this case, is absolutely the *sole* and adequate *cause* of the constitution of fundamental rights. In fact, this baptismal causality constitutes the moral faculties themselves or the substance of these rights. This causality, however, does not extend to the external structure of these rights, because the Church, by not recognizing baptism of this sort, places an obstacle from the outside which prevents the baptized from being coordinated with the faithful, as far as the constitution of rights through baptism is concerned, or from being incorporated into the Church or having the efficacious exercise of these rights.[42] Hence, the requisite external structure, an essential element of these rights, is not constituted; these rights are not completely constituted. Consequently, they have no juridical efficacy. For, although these rights are constituted through baptism as the vicarious action of Christ, Christ the Lord Himself made the Church the society which was entrusted with the administration of the economy of salvation on the supernatural order. These rights must, therefore, be applied and exercised within the Church. The salvific means necessary for the attainment of the supernatural end must be sought from the Church. Accordingly, the profession of faith and union with the Church is by

32

divine decree the most fundamental duty of the baptized. When this obligation is refused, the Church cannot recognize the baptism. For baptism is ordered to the constitution of the fundamental rights of the supernatural order, which are, however, to be exercised in the communion of the faithful, i.e., in the Church, a union in the charity of Christ through the Holy Spirit. These fundamental rights of the baptized cannot be totally and efficaciously constituted unless the baptized recognize this ecclesiological function.

Hence it is clear that, on the contrary, nothing else is required for the total constitution of these rights—presupposing valid baptism—except the profession of faith and communion with the Church. Given this profession, baptismal causality automatically extends to the constitution of the requisite external structure of these rights, namely, a structure which is assimilated within the Church, so that they can be efficaciously exercised.

The fundamental rights of the baptized can also be restricted by means of a *canonical penalty*. Such a restriction of rights on the part of the Church is to be explained in the same way as it was in the case of baptized non-Catholics: juridical efficacy is lacking in the exercise of rights as long as the rights are restricted, although the substance of the rights always remains.[43] For this substance inheres in the very sacramental character of the baptized and, therefore, cannot be lost. With the removal of the canonical penalty the efficacious exercise of rights can automatically be had again.

In the light of these statements it is clear that the fundamental rights of the baptized in accordance with the norms of Canon 87 are simply not possessed as long as the baptized refuse communion with the Church (here the

33

obstacle is the defect of profession of faith and communion with the Church), or are deprived of such communion by the Church by means of a canonical penalty.

What has been said here concerning the constitution of the fundamental rights of the baptized in the supernatural order applies also to the Church's influence upon the reception of sacred power to be exercised in the Church, the power which is sacramentally conferred and thus inheres in the ordained through the characters of orders as a quality of the soul. Nevertheless, a further explanation of this question forms the second part of this study.

CONCLUSIONS

Man, as a person, is a spiritual nature substantially joined to a body. Hence it is metaphysically necessary to distinguish between the internal structure and the external structure of human sociability.

1. There is an *internal structure* because human sociability is formally constituted by man's intentional relations that are specified and consequently distinguished by the common human good to which such relations are ordained. Social being is, therefore, internal to man and is an intentional being which, as all human goods, affords man personal perfection. The external structure of human sociability is constituted by the transposition of this internal structure to the outside, namely, its organization in external social life.

Since the internal structure of human sociability—constituted by the intentional relations of persons themselves—is by nature antecedent to and independent of (as spiritual and internal to man) every organized association, it cannot be affected by such an organization. Nevertheless, an organized association can affect the *external structure* of human sociability, because it is the function of an organized association to coordinate—for the common good—the exercise of man's fundamental rights and to incorporate this exercise into the social life. For this reason, an organized association has a duty to prevent the constitution of rights that are in opposition to the common good; consequently, it can place an obstacle that would render the formation of the external structure of rights impossible.

For human values are realized by the exercise of fundamental rights, namely, through a juridical act, i.e., through an intentional act that is externally manifested in order that a juridical effect may be had. The causality of a juridical act that has been rightly posited always creates the very right to be constituted *in its substance* (intentional being) and internal structure. But an obstacle can be placed to the formation of the external structure of this right by the fact that the *exercise* of a fundamental *right* in relation to the constitution of an acquired right is not recognized, because it is contrary to the common good. If such recognition is lacking, if, therefore, the requisite external structure of the right to be constituted is lacking, this right is not completely constituted and cannot be exercised.

2. By man's supernatural elevation even his sociability is elevated because his intentionality is essentially increased. Hence, it is metaphysically necessary to distinguish between the internal structure and the external structure of supernaturally elevated human sociability.

Man is made capable of efficaciously pursuing a supernatural end, of leading a supernatural life. For this purpose he is sealed with a baptismal character that inheres in his soul as an intentional being and unites him in a special way with Christ. Hence the *internal structure* of supernaturally elevated human sociability is constituted by the intentional relationships of the baptized that are based on the baptismal character and ordained to the actuation of particular supernatural values. And these values, as a whole, constitute the supernatural good in its totality as one out of the common human values (consequent to man's supernatural elevation) or, in other words, as the development of the very life of Christ the Lord among men. Since this internal structure of supernaturally elevated human sociability is had through Christ the Lord Himself —for baptism is the vicarious action of Christ—and since it is developed through the intentional acts of the baptized, it is internal to the baptized, rationally antecedent to the Church as a human society, and cannot be touched by it.

The *external structure* of supernaturally elevated human sociability is constituted by transposing this internal structure to the outside, i.e., by organization in the external social life which is, therefore, of a supernatural character, at least because of the end to which it is directed. Hence it is the Church's function, as an organized association, to coordinate the exercise of rights—in virtue of the common good—and to incorporate this exercise into the communion of the faithful or into the Church itself as a human society. For this reason the Church can truly influence the external structure of supernaturally elevated human sociability.

For, since all human activity is to be ordered to a supernatural end, supernatural human goods are realized through the exercise of fundamental rights both of the supernatural order as well as the natural. The *causality of a juridical act* that has been properly posited always creates the very right which is to be constituted in its substance or internal structure. The Church can, however, place an obstacle to

36

of Christ among men must be elaborated as the building
of the body of Christ which is the Church.

Notes

1. "Only those actions of which man is in control are called properly
human actions; but man is in control of his acts through his reason and
will . . . therefore those actions which proceed from a deliberate will are
said to be properly human actions" (St. Thomas, Summa Theol., I–II, q. 1,
a. 1 corp). "Man is said to have been made in the image of God, inasmuch
as the image signifies a being which is endowed with an intellect, free will
and power proper to it . . . inasmuch as man is also the principle of his
own actions, since he has a free will and power over his own actions"
(Ibid., Prologue). "This noun, intention, indicates the act of the will,
granted the ordination of reason disposing a thing to an end" (Ibid., q. 12,
a. 1, ad 3). "But only the created rational nature is immediately ordained
to God. . . . the rational nature, however, insofar as it knows the good and
being in their universal aspects, is immediately ordained to the universal
principle of being" (Summa Theol., II–II, q. 2, a. 3 corp. "Every intellectual
substance is in some way everything insofar as it is capable of compre-
hending all being with its intellect" (Summa contra Gent., III, c. 112,
5.) "The personal acts of a rational creature are in a proper sense acts
which belong to the rational soul" (Ibid., c. 113, 7).
2. "The internal structure of human social life consists in the union
of men since by their acts they develop their own personal perfection at
the same time as the entire human good which is based upon personality
itself" (G. Gundlach, S.J., "Annotationes ad nuntium radiophonicum Pii
XII. 24.12. 1942," Periodica de re morali, canonica, liturgica, 32 [1943],
82). "We must recognize objective 'common goods" (common values)
which teleologically constitute the internal structure of social life and, as
befits its spirituality, reduce it to 'a unity of order,' namely, the order of
one in many. First among those objective 'common goods' is human personality itself and its perfect development which is the internal end of
every man as the image of God. This value is not only the first but also the
foundation of the other 'common goods' (the various cultural and religious
values) in this sense that all those other 'common goods' and the unions
corresponding to them are destined to the service of the human person and
its development since the human person in being perfected is impelled to
the realization of those other goods according to their objective interdependence" (Ibid., 85). "The basis of society lies in man as a finite,
personal, spiritual substance, and as the image of God. . . . Since being
and value in their infinite totality are available and accessible within the
spirit, the spirit is by nature infinite. But since the human spiritual nature

is finite, this infinite totality is only potential to it. Whereas since this nature is also intentionality and coordination towards this infinite totality, this totality is also proper to it. Man always realizes that intentionality only in a finite and individual way, i.e., as a spiritual nature existing in matter, time and space. Considered as a whole, these factors form the basis of man's sociability and historicity. For he is spiritually accessible to all other men for the purpose of more perfectly realizing this intentionality. He depends upon coexistence with other men for his own self-realization. Formally sociability is the internal relationship and reciprocity of men which are the consequences of the explained ontological foundation. Sociability expresses man's common responsibility, which is based on personal value-intentionality, for the realization of the full value of being a man" (G. Gundlach, S.J., "Gesellschaft," *Staatslexikon*, Herausgegeben von der Görres-Gesellschaft, 3 Band [Freiburg, i.B., 1959⁶], c. 819.

3. "The origin and essential purpose of the social life is necessarily the conservation, development, and perfecting of the human person by assisting it to the proper observance of the norms and values of religion and culture" (Pius XII, "Nunt. radioph. 24.12. 1942," *Acta Apostolicae Sedis* 35 [1943], 12).

4. "Intentional being is an accident of finite, spiritual knowing and willing. The spiritual relationships of persons in the realization of these intentional values are of the same nature. The being of any social structure amounts to an 'intentional' being . . . to a real accident which has its source in the persons themselves, i.e., in the sociability which is rooted in their spiritual being and which appears in concrete life primarily as the norm-regulated co-relation of the actions of socially united individuals" (A. Rauscher, S.J., *Subsidiaritätsprinzip und berufsständische Ordnung in "Quadragesimo Anno"* [Münster i.W., 1958], pp. 27 f.). "The social life, therefore, has a true being, namely, an accidental, intentional being: the common spiritual relationship of persons to the unifying, common, super-individual value" (*Ibid.*, p. 39). "The relationships spiritually and necessarily join each individual, autonomous person with other persons in the realization of values. By reason of his nature every man is always intentionally close to and with all other men. This social coexistence is certainly not limited to the present alone. In virtue of the potential totality man is linked to the past and future as well, and stands in continuous relationship to all mankind" (A. Rauscher, S.J., "Die Relation-Kategorie des Sozialen," *Jahrbuch des Instituts für christliche Sozialwissenschaften* [Münster i.W., 1962], p. 55).

5. "Finally, it follows that sociability, as an inner coordination of persons, entails that the persons in their essential, spiritual-substantial entirety, in their self-possession and autonomy are subjects of rights endowed with the moral faculty for external freedom and, therefore, bearers of personal rights. Herein lies the basis for the interior connection of human sociability with the natural law" (G. Gundlach, "Gesellschaft," *Staatslexikon*, cc. 819 f.).

6. "The body is ontologically an essential part of man, and is as equally necessary to the full man as his spiritual soul. The body provides the soul with the realm of activity that is due to it and makes possible its development in space and time in the visible world. . . . It gives the flowing spiritual life the sturdy framework that is indispensable for its operation in space and time. But only if this framework is exclusively seized and stamped by the spirit, only if it remains a framework and does not set itself up as an end in itself, only if it does not wish to violate and to measure according to its own standards its contents, i.e., the spiritual life, but remains in helpful readiness and subordination, in helpful self-moderation, does it fulfil its natural destiny, that of being part of the essence of man and nothing else" (Rauscher, *Subsidiaritätsprinzip*, p. 21). "The human person is rather the spirit that comes into being and lives in the spatio-temporal corporeality. The spiritual soul does not develop still 'further conceptual relationships,' but is necessarily realized as a human spirit in the organic material life as well. Hence this life can never come into conflict with the spiritual life, since it is itself the spirit realizing itself in historicity, and in its unity and ontological totality it belongs to man as the particular image of God" (*Ibid.*, p. 29).

7. Recognition must be given to organized institutions and unions that express in the external order the relationships of both physical and moral persons, the relationships which result from the internal structure of social life. This is intrinsically necessary since we are dealing with the social life of human beings, i.e., beings composed of body and soul and living in space and time" (Gundlach, "Annotationes,"*Periodica de re morali, canonica, liturgica,* 85). The external structure shows the organization of society and its life. We are not dealing here with some addition from the external to the internal structure, but with something without which human society cannot be a reality and above all the dynamic reality of history. The organization of social life is the necessary projection into corporeality, into space and time, that is to say, the realization of the contents of sociability" (Gundlach, "Gesellschaft," *Staatslexikon,* c. 820). "Naturally the conditioning factor of pure possibility of being is also realized in this correlation of man. It does not come 'as an addition' to an already subsisting relation, but invests it with a quasi corporeo-spatio-temporal dimension. On the one hand there are the human values which the potentially total autonomy of man is destined to realize. Marriage, family, economy, architecture, music, science—all of these are human values and as such are endowed with a corporeo-spatio-temporal reality. On the other hand the sociability which is based upon intentionality needs a so-to-speak corporeal organization in order to become a human society. The State, international, territorial, and professional organizations, as well as marriage and the family cannot exist without an organized legal structure. Finally the realization of intentional relations is accomplished not in eternal timelessness, but in the historical sequence of time and in concrete space" (Rauscher, *art. cit., Jahrbuch des Instituts für christliche Socialwissenschafts,* p. 55).

8. Gundlach, "Annotationes," *Periodica de re morali, canonica, liturgica,* p. 87.

9. Cf. Pius XI, Encyclical, *Divini Redemptoris, Acta Apostolicae Sedis* 29 (1937), 78 f. Pius XII, "Nunt. radioph. 24.12. 1942," *A.A.S.* 35 (1943), 17–19. H. Meyer, *Sittlichkeit, Recht und Staat* (Paderborn, 1960), pp. 416 ff. These fundamental human rights are based directly upon man's personality. Hence they are of their nature antecedent to organized society, be it concrete or abstract.

10. Because he is ordered to God man forms an absolute, inviolable value which is the basis for the absolute value of fundamental rights.

11. "The opinions are rejected (in the radio address) which assert that the structure of social life arises from organized unions and institutions or from the external order, and this in such a way that they do not admit an internal order of social life in addition to the external order, or deny that the external order intrinsically and necessarily follows upon the internal order of which it is the necessary external formation (organization) since we are dealing with the social life of composite, not purely spiritual, beings. Such views reduce the structure of the social life and its formal cause to an institution of the juridical order, to the State as to a concentrated power (force), to organizational forms in general. . . . The opinions are rejected which identify or confuse the internal order of social life with the external order. This amounts to the same thing as not distinguishing between the goods (values) concerning which and because of which social life is established, internally structured, or diversified with various unions, and the organizational good of social life, whether as a whole or as a particular. This is the same as confusing "the common goods" and "the common good" by paying no attention to the fact that "the common goods," namely, the objective ends of social life (e.g., in economy, science, arts, and religion) are to be referred to the internal structure of social life, whereas "the common good" constitutes the objective end of the external order of that life, and hence indicates organizational finality which therefore supposes and follows what is to be organized, namely, the social life and its internal structure together with "the common goods" (values) and the various unions which are intentionally had concerning them" (Gundlach, "Annotationes," *Periodica de re morali, canonica, liturgica* [1943], 83 f.

12. "The eternal law is nothing else than an aspect of the divine wisdom inasmuch as it is directive of all actions and movements" (St. Thomas, *Summa theol.,* I–II, q. 93, a. 1 corp). Cf. also *De Veritate,* q. 23, a. 6.

13. "Every organization has two elements: administration and a system of rules of conduct. Consequently, it is on this level that realities are met such as authority on the one hand, and positive law, rules of ethics, custom, and convention on the other. Authority and every other element of power and every rule of conduct are always situated within the internal conceptual relationship of the value-intentionality which establishes and perfects society. Proceeding on the assumption that the preservation of

the internal structure of sociability in its permanent realization is a concern of everyone as a person and in this sense belongs to the common good, then the organization of social life must be irrevocably and above all directed to this point. As an organizational function, the application of administration and rules of conduct, when it has been so adapted, and is immediately directed to the preservation of sociability as such, is the common good" (Gundlach, "Gesellschaft," *Staatslexikon*, 820 f.). *The common good in the technical sense* is therefore referred to *the organization of social life.*

14. The state—as every organized association—is of its nature characterized as a moral person. Although a moral person acts by means of physical persons, it is itself—since it constitutes an intentional and teleological unity—the subject of rights and duties. Cf. my study: "De personalitatis moralis in iure canonico natura metaphysica," *Periodica de re morali, canonica, liturgica*, 48 (1959), 213 ff.

15. The common good, therefore, should be devoted to the realization of common human goods. The common good requires such organization in social life to insure the peaceful and orderly exercise of every person's— physical and moral persons—rights. Order and peace in social life are results of the common good which is devoted to the personal perfection of all as a group.

16. "The juridical order is not, as it were, a piece of clothing, an external accretion to man's social life. Rather it is the necessary formation (an institutive organization) of the internal structure of social life which is, and because it is certainly the spiritual life of beings composed of soul and body and necessarily living in time and space. Hence we must reject juridical Positivism which denies the internal and essential structure of social life and looks for the source of the juridical order on the outside. . . . We reject the same juridical positivism which destroys the internal unity of the juridical order since it does not recognize the ontological foundation of this unity, namely, the internal structure of social life. . . . The establishment of true clarity and security along with the capacity for adaptation in the juridical order, as required by the quality of the reality just indicated, is achieved only when the source of the juridical order is considered to be in the internal structure of social life. For that structure contains strictly immutable relationships which must, nevertheless, of their very nature be constantly applied, and are applicable to concrete mutable relationships. . . . The importance of the juridical order for the social life cannot be sufficiently stressed. For any true juridical relationship aims at the liberty which is due to a moral or physical person according to its own essential end. Consequently, through organization, the juridical order aims at the realization of the internal structure of social life." (Gundlach, "Annotationes," *Periodica de re morali, canonica, liturgica*, 32 [1943], 89–92).

17. Cf. O. Robleda, S.J., "Nullitas actus iuridici in *Codice Iuris Canonici*," *Periodica de re morali, canonica, liturgica*, 35 (1946), 29 ff.

18. "Since the agent's will, which is essential to the facts of the

declaratory act, is called a will to effect legal consequences, it is immediately evident that the object of the agent's conscious striving is the legal consequences of his act. Hence we can dispose of those earlier, much discussed opinions which proposed that the agent has to strive only for actual and economic consequences which are then made into legal consequences by law. These views, which are connected with the theory of automatic release (*Auslösungstheorie*) discussed above, were based upon a complete misunderstanding of personal autonomy as a function of law" (A. Manigk, *Das rechtswirksame Verhalten* [Berlin, 1939] p. 145). Cf. on this question O. Robleda, S.J., "De conceptu actus iuridici," *Periodica de re morali, canonica, liturgica*, 51 (1962), 413 ff., especially 437 ff. According to our assertions, organized society exerts influence upon the efficacy of the juridical activity of persons. Hence, as we have said, when such a society blocks the efficacy of a right, the external structure of the right to be constituted, or already substantially constituted, cannot be formed. Other authors also maintain that an organized association can block the juridical efficacy of the juridical acts of persons because such a faculty is required by natural law. But they maintain rather that there is not even any influence on the very internal structure of juridical acts, and that lack of recognition on the part of the organized association is sufficient to explain a juridical act which is really existent, but juridically inefficacious.

19. B. Durst, O.S.B., "De characteribus sacramentalibus," *Xenia Thomistica* II (Romae, 1925) 541 ff.

20. "As His (Christ's) personal life as the God-Man represents the union of the divine and human, so should His living presence in society, notwithstanding the higher full effect of the divine in time and space, also imply the full development of mankind in history, of its individuals and communities in harmonious totality with the divine. In this sense, which comprehends the divine and the human, we speak of the living Christ, and we call His social extension, or rather the universal collectivity that results from the common acknowledgement of this living Christ, the Church" (G. Gundlach, S.J., *Zur Soziologie der katholischen Ideenwelt und des Jesuitenordens* [Freiburg i.B., 1927], p. 49).

21. Religion holds the first place among the common human values. In the concrete supernatural order the supernatural good also includes supernatural religion. The supernatural good of worship is, therefore, simultaneously a personal, human perfection.

22. "The Church which, according to Catholic dogma, was instituted by Christ is itself a social unit and, therefore, exhibits all the ontological properties of the internal and external structure and purpose of society. But the Church possesses all of these in a new, blessed, supernatural way and with an intensity and profundity not naturally due to man as a creature, of his image-of-Godliness, his personal being and value with the concomitantly given sociability and historicity in their whole human substance. Thus, then, the intentional being that is characteristic of the Church, as of every society, also implies a social reality of unheard-of

43

originality, built upon the equally unheard-of, expanded dimension of the value-intentionality of the human spiritual beings redeemed by Christ and joined with Him in oneness of life. Now if this Church which, as a society, has arisen only from the gracious will of God and which has as its special objective the salvation of man is compared with the whole of human society, thus with the whole of mankind, then the point of contact for both social structures is the human person in virtue of this person's value-intentionality that forms the basis of sociability and historicity. For this reason the contact of both structures is of an internal nature and, as with contact in social life in general, is a correlationship, an internal co-existence, whereby the Church gives of her particular, more noble vital energy. This is the meaning when one calls the Church a vital principle of human society. This excludes an organizational misinterpretation, as well as all religious integralism, because every sphere of values in the internal and external structure of society remains steadfast in its respective inner laws" (G. Gundlach, S.J., "Gesellschaft," *Staatslexikon*, col. 842).

23. A cleric or the clerical office is understood in this section in a general sense. That is to say, it is used here for those of the faithful who possess power, sacramentally given by Christ the Lord, in the Church with a view to the supernatural good and end. There is no specification of the degree of hierarchical orders that would be required for this.

24. "The successors of the Apostles are endowed with the Holy Spirit. Consequently, their power is ultimately divine not only in origin but also in essence" (M. Kaiser, *Die Einheit der Kirchengewalt nach dem Zeugnis des Neuen Testamentes und der Apostolischen Väter* [München, 1956], p. 138).

25. "The power of orders is referred to the true body of Christ the Lord in the sacred Eucharist . . . and includes everything else that can in any way be referred to the Eucharist" (*Catechismus SS. Conc. Tridentini ad Parochos* [Bassani, 1833], Cap. VII, 6 f.).

26. The power of jurisdiction is the Church's moral faculty of directing the activity of the faithful to the supernatural end. "For it is its function to govern and guide the Christian people, and to direct them to eternal and celestial beatitude"; it "is completely concerned with the Mystical Body of Christ," i.e., it is referred to the Church as a social body. *Catech. Trident., loc. cit.*—This power is concerned "with the actions of men that, with the help of God's grace, the necessary cooperation of the faithful themselves may be had through the true profession of faith and conformity of life to Christian morals. . . . But the power which belongs to the Church for the governing of men, i.e., for the authoritative direction of their acts both in faith and in morals, is called the power of jurisdiction" (A. Cardinal Ottaviani, *Institutiones Iuris Publici Ecclesiastici*, I [Typ. Pol. Vat., 1958[4]], 178 f.). "The governing power, which directs and manages growth in the Church springs from the same root from which the life of the new people of God springs and by it is constantly renewed and kept alive. This one root is Jesus Christ, the productive foundation of the new

people of God. He is at one and the same time the lifegiving and regulating principle of this people" (Kaiser, op. cit., p. 41). "Teaching, as any other function of the successors of the Apostles, was integrated into the universal mandate which they had received from the Apostles and in virtue of which they occupied a position of authority in the community" (Ibid., p. 131).

27. Only clerics can have power of orders or power of jurisdiction (Can. 118). Our only point in this context is that the power of Christ which is transmitted to clerics presupposes the reception of sacred ordination. We prescind from the other questions which arise under this heading.

28. The priesthood of Christ is here understood as His office of mediator between God and men and also includes His office of king and prophet.

29. "But they are utterly wrong in introducing a distinction of this sort (between the Church of charity and the Church of law). For they do not understand that the divine Redeemer had the same motive for wishing the body of men which He founded to be established as a society, perfect of its kind, and to be provided with all of the juridical and social elements, namely, that He might continue the salvific work of Redemption on this earth (Pius XII, Encyclical, Mystici Corporis Christi, Acta Apostolicae Sedis 35 [1943], 224).

30. Cf. supra, n. 22.

31. These functions are accomplished by the power of jurisdiction; cf. supra, n. 26.

32. Thus, e.g., the administration of the Church's temporal goods is ordered to the Church's supernatural life which can exist among men only in a human way. Hence temporal goods are also required to carry on the life of the Church; because of the end which they serve their administration for the good of the Church possesses a supernatural quality.

33. The exercise of the power of orders is regulated by the power of jurisdiction. A liturgical law is established by the power of jurisdiction. Yet frequently the power of orders and the power of jurisdiction simultaneously cooperate in the same activity, e.g., in sacramental absolution.

34. Consequently, the entire social life of the Church is regulated by the power of jurisdiction.

35. We must note, however, that social activity does not always possess this supernatural quality in the same "degree." It is most present in that activity which directly expresses the supernatural, internal life of the Church in an external way, as in the Eucharistic Sacrifice; and also in that activity which directly, ex opere operato, produces the supernatural life in an external way, as in the sacraments. Such a supernatural quality is clearly obvious as well in the preaching of the Word of God, in the profession of faith, in the sanctification of holy days, in exhorting the faithful, clerics and religious to a Christian and more perfect life, in works of charity, etc. Finally the very administration of temporal goods ought to be devoted to the Church's supernatural end.

36. "By virtue of the juridical mission by which He sent His Apostles

45

into the world, just as He Himself was sent by the Father, our Divine Savior baptizes, teaches, governs, looses, binds, consecrates, and sacrifices through the Church. But in virtue of that higher, utterly interior and sublime gift that we earlier touched upon in describing how the Head influences its members, Christ our Lord bids the Church to live His own heavenly life and fills its entire Body with His divine power, and He nourishes and sustains each member according to his place in the Body, as the vine nourishes and makes fruitful the branches united to it.

"But if we carefully examine this divine principle of life and power given by Christ, insofar as it constitutes the very source of every gift and created grace, we understand that it is nothing else than the Paraclete, the Spirit who proceeds from the Father and the Son, and who is called in a special way 'the Spirit of Christ' or 'the Spirit of the Son.' . . . But after Christ is once glorified on the Cross, His Spirit is communicated to the Church with lavish prodigality that she and her individual members may be daily more and more like our Savior." (Encyclical, *Mystici Corporis Christi*, AAS 35 [1943], 218 f.). "For although the juridical principles which also support and organize the Church are derived from the divine constitution given by Christ and contribute to the pursuit of the celestial end, nevertheless, what lifts Christian society to an order completely surpassing every natural order is the Spirit of our Redeemer, who as the source of all graces, gifts, and charisms constantly permeates the Church and is active within her" (*Ibid.*, p. 223).

37. Cf. *supra*, pp. 23 f.

38. We are prescinding in this context from rights which might be constituted by the Church on its own authority.

39. It is clear that on these suppositions nothing prevents the sanation of a marriage which is invalid because of a lack of canonical form if, after a naturally valid and still existing consent, absolute and perpetual impotency should occur. Actually such a sanation has been granted more than once by the Holy See. On this subject confer my articles: "De effectu consensus matrimonialis naturaliter validi," *Miscellanea in memoriam Petri Cardinalis Gasparri* (Romae: Pont. Univ. Lateranensis, 1960), pp. 133 f. "De efficacitate consensus matrimonialis naturaliter validi," *Periodica de re morali, canonica, liturgica*, 51 (1962), 295 ff.

40. The Church acts in this way, e.g., in establishing invalidating and disqualifying laws. On the question of whether—in the case of the invalidation of an act or disqualification of a person—the juridical act is inefficacious because of the prescription as such of ecclesiastical authority, which should be endowed with this power because of the end given it by Christ our Lord, or is it rather that in such a case there is a lack of the external structure requisite for the constitution of a right, confer *supra* n. 18. Furthermore it must be noted that the exercise of rights is also considered unlawful if other preceptive and prohibitive laws are violated. When, however, there is no invalidation of the act or disqualification of the person, the act is valid, although illicit.

41. Canon 87. It should be noted that in this discussion *the juridical effects* of baptism are in question. Hence there is no denial of the fact that through baptism a union is constituted between the baptized and Christ our Lord, the sign of which is the baptismal character. Nor is there any denial that baptism under the necessary suppositions confers *sanctifying grace*. Such questions, however, that are concerned with *the subjective condition of the baptized* must be distinguished from *questions* on the effects of baptism in the Church as an external juridical society that are connected rather with *the objective constitution of the Church*.

Furthermore, baptized non-catholics have received with baptism the faculty of acting supernaturally in its substance, and this inheres in the character. Hence, if they properly receive other sacraments, they are validly received, e.g., penance, extreme unction. For the principal efficient cause in the sacraments is Christ our Lord; the minister acts with instrumental causality. Moreover, under the necessary suppositions, the Church recognizes the juridical effects of the acts of baptized non-catholics. Thus, for example, their valid marriage is also a sacrament.

42. "But only those are to be really numbered among the members of the Church who have received baptism and profess the true faith and who have not unfortunately separated themselves from the structure of the Body, or been severed from it by legitimate authority because of very grave faults" (Pius XII, Encyclical, *Mystici Corporis Christi*, A.A.S. 35 [1943], 202). Therefore only those of the baptized who profess the true faith and union with the Catholic Church are here considered *members of the Church*. Consequently, the infants of Catholic parents are baptized within the faith of the Church. If this passage of the Encyclical is compared with Canon 87, it should be said that all the baptized are endowed with a *personality* of the supernatural order, a personality within the Church as well. (Moreover, they could not have the obligations of Christians if they were not persons in the juridical order.) Nevertheless, those who do not enjoy the profession of faith and communion with the Catholic Church, do not have the *exercise* of these rights. Those persons who have the exercise of these rights are considered members of the Church. It is not enough (for membership) that these rights be substantially constituted; rather it is necessary that the baptized be incorporated within the Church, that these rights be completely constituted. (These rights cannot be considered inefficacious in baptized non-catholics because their efficient causality is invalidated by the Church; for baptism, when validly received, always gives rise to the baptismal character in which the substance of these rights inheres. Hence, these rights which are substantially constituted by baptism must be inefficacious because the Church blocks their external structure. Confer *supra* nn. 18 and 40). But no further treatment can be given to the question of the members of the Church in this context.

43. The supernatural values that the Church denies the sinner are supernatural values as humanly possessed, i.e., as they are in the power of the Church. "What the Church can in no way communicate or touch,

such as grace and merits, she can in no way take away" (Vermeesch and Creusen, *Epitome Iuris Canonici*, III [Mechliniae: 1936[5]], 236). As a matter of fact there is no canonical penalty which cannot be explained in this way. (We are prescinding from rights that might be established by the Church and taken away as a penalty.) The exercise of rights is, therefore, more or less restricted by means of canonical penalty. Actually there is a specific restriction in the concrete for every species of penalty. If rights are simply removed—and this occurs at least in *excommunicatio vitandi*—the subject's juridical condition is the same as that of the baptized non-catholics. Therefore, rights are removed to the same extent as their exercise is no longer incorporated within the Church. Hence the exercise is invalid. (This statement is made on the supposition that the penalty removes the valid exercise of a right, not that it renders its exercise only illicit.)

Part II: *The Metaphysical Structure of the Episcopal Office*

Christ the Lord entrusted to His Church the administration of the economy of salvation on the supernatural order. Hence He left to the Church His power to fulfill such a function. This office is fulfilled through clerics, namely, through the faithful upon whom sacred ordination is sacramentally conferred for this purpose. Prescinding from all the other questions which arise under this heading, we shall here discuss only the relationship of the episcopal office to the primatial office, or the relationship between the episcopacy and the primacy, two offices which are certainly of divine right.

1. Historical Prenotes on the Conferral of the Episcopal Office

Although there are still many unsolved problems concerning the historical development of the relationship between the episcopacy and the primacy, these questions do not concern us in the present context.

We would merely like to note that the *prohibition of absolute ordination* is of great importance to our problem. Absolute ordination is the conferral of ordination upon a candidate who does not receive at the time a sacred office in a determined church. Until the end of the twelfth century ordination always had to be conferred for a determined church. The conferral of ordination and the conferral of the sacred office, therefore, were lawfully accomplished by one single act, namely ordination itself.[1]

It is true of course that in the early days of the Church there were missionaries who exercised the office of preaching while travelling from place to place. Nevertheless, the Apostles were already placing over the Christian communities ordained men who permanently exercised the sacred office in that Christian community.[2] In post-apostolic times ordination for a determined Christian community or particular church was the rule. As the organization of the local Church was perfected, itinerant missionaries were less in evidence. It is not possible to assert positively that there were no ordinations in the second and third centuries in which the ordained did not assume a sacred office in a particular church. It is, however, an established fact that from the fourth century on at any rate absolute ordinations became more frequent. Absolute ordinations disrupted ecclesiastical discipline, i.e., ecclesiastical life under the vigilance of the bishops. For a cleric ordained in such a manner had no bishop to whom he was subject in the exercise of the power received through ordination. He was acephalous, a wanderer (vagus). Although the Church was not favorably disposed towards clerics who were absolutely ordained, absolute ordinations could not be completely excluded. Thus, for example, absolute ordination was practiced among the monks.[3]

Finally, the Ecumenical Council of Chalcedon strictly forbade absolute ordinations in 451.[4] While this prohibition was in force, absolute ordinations still continued to occur

And so the doctrine, now common for centuries, developed. It principally distinguishes between the power that is present in a subject through the valid reception of ordination and consequently can always be validly exercised, and the power which, although ordination was validly received, is not yet present in the subject and consequently cannot be validly exercised. According to this doctrine, moreover, the valid exercise of sacred power can still be unlawful, i.e., illicit. When ordination is validly performed, the subject possesses the power of orders which can always be validly, although perhaps illicitly, exercised. The power of jurisdiction, however, is no longer joined to ordination as such.

The prohibition of absolute ordination had great bearing on the question of *episcopal consecration*. The primitive Church looked up to bishops as subjects of the sacred power which the Apostles received from Christ and passed on to their successors as the power of Christ.[8] Even though this power extended to worship, preaching the word of God, and governing, it was viewed completely as a unit that was conferred through the imposition of hands.[9] The imposition of hands, however, had to be conferred for a determined church. Otherwise, since he was without a proper office, the ordinee was not considered a bishop.[10] Absolute ordination was not permitted in the case of a bishop. Indeed, the connection between the bishop and his church was considered indissoluble. Consequently the transfer of bishops from one see to another were *de se* excluded.[11]

Therefore, by episcopal consecration for a particular, determined church the ordinee received together with such consecration not only the sacred power but also the execution of the sacred power, a power which constituted a unit as described. He received the exercise of the power of the episcopal order and the exercise of the power of governing or jurisdiction (as we would say today). On the other hand, if the episcopal consecration was absolute, the sacred power was considered "void": neither the power of orders could be lawfully exercised nor was the exercise of jurisdiction possessed.

We have, therefore, on the one hand the practice of the ancient Church. It held that, together with episcopal consecration for a particular determined church, there was conferred the Episcopal office, i.e., the execution not only of the power of orders but also of the power of governing in the Church. It maintained, however, that this office was not conferred with absolute episcopal consecration although such a consecration could not be considered simply invalid (i.e., as if it never took place). On the other hand we have the contemporary practice of the Church. According to this, jurisdiction that can be exercised is not conferred with episcopal consecration as such. Episcopal consecration does, however, always confer the power of orders and its valid exercise.

The ancient and contemporary practices of the Church ought to be reduced to principles that explain both practices. Consequently, we can say: In the light of the practice of the ancient and contemporary Church, as well as the common teaching of the Church that the episcopacy is an office divinely established to govern in the Church, we legitimately assume that the episcopal office of governing in the Church is conferred through episcopal consecration, but that the episcopal consecration as such does not confer the exercise of this jurisdiction. This means that the power of governing in the Church is also sacramentally constituted in a concrete subject by the conferral of the episcopal office, but that the exercise of this jurisdiction is not had by the divine conferral of the episcopal office. We explicitly note that we do not intend to prove these statements here; rather we assume them; that is to say, we assume that the episcopal office of governing in the Church is sacramentally conferred. From the very beginning the constant tradition in the Church has been that this office is constituted by episcopal consecration. And this tradition is not destroyed by the development of the reflex distinction of sacred power into the power of orders and the power of jurisdiction, although this development has need of some explanation.[12] Furthermore, what shall be said here is of itself independent of the mode[13] by which the episcopal office, divine in instituion and conferral, is acquired by a subject.

In the light of these prenotes and presuppositions, therefore, we say:

The episcopal office of governing in the Church is conferred upon a concrete subject through episcopal consecration. To exercise the office of governing in the Church, however, the divinely established and sacramentally conferred power of governing in the Church must be coordinated with the power of governing possessed by the other bishops. This coordination belongs to the Roman Pontiff.

2. SUBSTANCE AND EFFICACY OF THE EPISCOPAL OFFICE

The episcopacy is the divinely established office of "tending the flock of God" (1 Pet. 5:2), of "ruling the Church of God" (Acts 20:28). Hence the episcopal office is made up of the "office" of tending God's flock and of the power necessary to fulfill this function, i.e., the power of governing God's Church. The episcopal office is first of all an "office" or obligation and, because of the "office," power is inherent in it. This power is the power of Christ the Lord entrusted to the Church. For this reason the episcopal office is rightly considered the plenitude of the priesthood.[14] This fullness of the priesthood, therefore, contains not only the power of orders but also, indeed especially, the power of governing in the Church. The power of governing in the Church is related to the universal Church, at least insofar as the bishop acts in communion with the rest of the bishops (in an Ecumenical Council). In a special way, however, this power of governing in the Church is referred to a particular church, i.e., a community in the Church, a part of the universal Church.[15] Consequently, all the essential constitutive elements of the episcopal office are present when an episcopal consecration has been properly performed. Hence, the episcopal office is existent in its substance, its intentional being, and its internal structure within a concrete subject.

The internal structure of the episcopal office results from its ordination to the celebration of worship, the sanctification of the faithful (especially, through the sacraments), the preservation and proclamation of the teaching which Christ the Lord transmitted to His Church, the imposition and application of the precepts that Christ the Lord left to His Church, and everything necessary or suitable (proper) for the possession of these supernatural goods. Therefore, the faculties (power and rights) and the "offices" proper to the episcopal office are related to the internal structure of the episcopal office. These faculties and "offices" are possessed in their intentional being, since they are constituted by intentional relations to the baptized which are determined by the supernatural goods just mentioned. Truly therefore, this substance of the episcopal office is constituted by a properly performed episcopal

55

consecration. (Although, of course, the power of the Church as previously explained constitutes a unity, in the following remarks when we speak of the episcopal office we are especially referring to the faculties [powers and rights] of teaching and governing in the Church, i.e., the jurisdictional element of the episcopal office. In these pages we shall briefly designate such powers as the episcopal office or power of governing.)

It should be indicated, therefore, that this power of governing is related to the internal structure of supernaturally elevated human sociability. For this power is possessed by a concrete subject, a concrete person, and constitutes a quality of the consecrated person. The concrete subject is consecrated by episcopal consecration or, in other words, is sanctified by the activity of Christ the Lord to exercise episcopal functions. For this reason the subject who has been sanctified for this purpose is marked with this power along with the episcopal character in which it inheres. Just as the fundamental rights of the baptized substantially inhere in the baptismal character, so the power of governing in the Church substantially inheres in the episcopal character. Just as the fundamental rights of the baptized are substantially possessed from the union with Christ constituted through baptism, so the power of governing in the Church is substantially possessed through participation in the sacred power of Christ, the Mediator of the New Testament, a participation which is constituted through episcopal consecration. Just as the fundamental rights of the baptized are substantially possessed, rationally antecedent to the Church as a human society, so this power of governing is substantially possessed, rationally antecedent to the Church as a human society. For the sacraments are vicarious actions of Christ.

Hence power of a supernatural character, in particular the bishop's power of governing, is substantially and truly conferred in the episcopal consecration as the vicarious action of Christ rationally antecedent to the Church as a human society. Nevertheless, such power is ordered to the Church as a human society.

Actually such power is to be exercised in the Church as a human society. For this power, established in its internal structure, cannot—as any faculty of social activity among men who are made up of soul and body—be exercised as long as it lacks an external structure. Especially because of the bishop's power of governing, or rather because of the exercise of the power of governing, the internal structure of sociability cannot be without an *external structure* or organization. The internal and external life of the Church —insofar as the latter is had in social and juridical activity— are a unit. Its internal life is completed by external activity, so that it may be truly human. Through external activity the internal life is transposed to the outside, made manifest, perfected, and operative.

Hence, the episcopal office, conferred in its internal structure in the act of consecration, needs an external structure by means of which *it is incorporated within the Church.* For this office is to be exercised within the Church in which there are other bishops who enjoy the same power. If they have no order in the exercise of this office, this exercise is not for the good of the social whole which the Church constitutes; it is of no use for the building of the Body of Christ but for its destruction. Therefore, the exercise of the power of all bishops must be coordinated with a view to governing in the Church, with a view to the possession of the Church's common good. There must be a *communion of all the bishops* who exercise episcopal power in the Church. Just as the coordination of the baptized (because of the ordination of their activity to a supernatural end) is necessary for the efficacious realization of the exercise of their fundamental rights on the natural and supernatural orders, so coordination is also necessary for the peaceful and efficacious possession of the exercise of episcopal power on the part of all bishops for the common good of the Church and the building of the Body of Christ.

Hence it is that episcopal consecration as such does not satisfy all that is required to grant the consecrated bishop the actual exercise of his episcopal power in the Church. The constitution and conferral of the power of governing in the Church are not as such sufficient for the exercise of this power. Although the episcopal office is possessed substantially and existentially by means of episcopal consecration, the divine constitution and sacramental conferral of the episcopal office in its substance do not as such bring about communion with the rest of the bishops. The common good of the Church as a human society—since it is a society with an external life and organization, an essential part of its life and intimately connected with its internal life—demands that the conferral of the episcopal office through consecration must be recognized by the Church for the exercise of the office in the Church. Such recognition brings about communion with the rest of the bishops and coordination of the exercise of the newly consecrated bishop's power with the exercise of power on the part of all the other bishops. When this recognition is lacking, the conferral and reception of the episcopal office lack "the canonical form," which is demanded because of the common good, for the exercise of this office in the Church. When this "canonical form," namely, recognition on the part of the Church of the episcopal office, is lacking, the episcopal office which has been duly constituted in its substance and existence, in its internal structure, by episcopal consecration, lacks the external structure legally *required* in the Church. And when this structure is lacking, this office is not completely constituted and, consequently, is not efficaciously possessed nor can it be exercised.

Doubtless episcopal consecration, as the efficient cause of the episcopal office, not only creates the internal structure of the episcopal office, but also is capable of creating its external structure. Furthermore, in the case of the episcopal office, the external structure is the transposition and formation on the outside of the internal structure, so that, of itself, the causality of the consecration automatically extends to the creating of the external structure of the episcopal office. Nevertheless, it is the Church's function, as an organized society to which every institution of the supernatural order is entrusted, to coordinate the exercise of power on the part of all the bishops, so that order and peace may be established and preserved in the life of the Church. Hence it is the Church's function *to recognize* the conferral (through episcopal consecration) of the episcopal office for the incorporation of the consecrated bishop within the hierarchy of the Church. Consequently when this recognition of episcopal consecration is lacking, the episcopal office lacks juridical efficacy, i.e., efficacy in the Church as an external and juridical society. The Church, therefore, by not recognizing the juridical efficacy of an episcopal consecration prevents the causality of episcopal consecration, as regards episcopal power, from extending to the external structure of episcopal power. Therefore, although the Church cannot affect the causality as such of the episcopal consecration itself—since it is the vicarious action of Christ—it can and ought to be able to affect this causality inasmuch as such causality touches the external, social, juridical life of the Church, i.e., inasmuch as the substantially conferred episcopal power is to be exercised in the Church as an external and juridical society, or in other words inasmuch as such power becomes efficacious. Wherefore, because the efficacy of the episcopal power, which is of itself substantially conferred in episcopal consecration, is not recognized, an obstacle is externally placed so that the internal structure of the episcopal office may not be transposed to the outside. Consequently, the external structure of the episcopal office cannot be formed.

When the external structure of the episcopal office is lacking, this office is without its "body." An essential element is missing; the office is, as a result, not completely constituted in a concrete subject although it is possessed in its substance or internal structure. For this reason, therefore, the recognition of the conferral of the episcopal office by the Church is not the efficient cause of power. This is rather the result of episcopal consecration. Recognition of the conferral of the episcopal office is the *condition* that must be fulfilled for the possession of the *juridical* efficacy of the conferral of the office and consequently of the efficacy of the office itself. Yet this condition is essential because, when it is not fulfilled, an obstacle is present that prevents the formation of an essential element, namely, the external structure of the episcopal office. So it is true, even in the case of the episcopal office, that of itself the external structure is formed automatically with the internal structure. Yet from the demonstration of a need for the fulfillment of an essential condition, i.e., recognition on the part of the Church, there follows a pressing need for adaptation of the episcopal office to the Church; there follows a pressing need for *that* external structure that is the sole manner in which the episcopal office is considered incorporated within the Church. When this external structure is lacking, the bishop is not in communion with the hierarchy of the Church, so that as a result, he cannot efficaciously exercise his power; therefore, the episcopal office is not completely constituted; therefore, the episcopal office is simply not possessed. The obstacle to the formation of the external structure of the episcopal office is consequently extrinsic to the efficient cause of the episcopal office, i.e., episcopal consecration. To have such structure, nothing more is required than the fulfillment of the condition legally placed by the Church. When the condition is fulfilled, the causality of consecration automatically extends to the creation of the external structure of the episcopal office. The external structure is present; juridical efficacy is present; the completely constituted episcopal office is present.

Hence it is clear that the conferral of the episcopal office can truly be compared with the conferral of the fundamental rights of the supernatural order on a concrete subject through baptism.[16] These rights are conferred in their substance and existence, in their intentional being and internal structure, by every valid baptism. For they inhere in the baptismal character and, consequently, cannot be lost. Nevertheless baptized non-catholics, since they place an obstacle, namely, the lack of profession of faith or communion with the Church, do not have communion with the Church. Hence their rights lack recognition on the part of the Church; they lack the external structure required in the Church as an external and juridical society, so that they are not completely constituted. Accordingly, these rights lack efficacy and, consequently, cannot be exercised. By the very fact, however, that the profession of faith and communion with the Church are made, the obstacle is removed so that such rights are completely constituted.

Similarly the bishop who has been duly consecrated (through episcopal consecration) sacramentally possesses in substance the power of governing in the Church. The episcopal office is an existent one because it is sacramentally conferred and inheres in the episcopal character. Yet, because of the lack of proper communion with the rest of the bishops (from the point of view of the exercise of the power of governing), or by reason of the lack of incorporation within the hierarchy of government, the episcopal office lacks its requisite external structure in the Church. Consequently, the episcopal power remains inefficacious; the exercise of the power of governing is not possessed. Thus it truly can and ought to be said that the episcopal power is simply not possessed.

Furthermore, in some true sense it can and ought to be said that the recognition of a bishop on the part of the Church also contributes something to the episcopal office in the line of causality. There is nothing corresponding to this element among the rights of the baptized. Nonetheless, this element is required for the episcopal office because the power of governing requires subjects who are under such power. Hence it must be said that, although the episcopal office has been completely constituted in a concrete subject, the bishop, nevertheless, has not yet been assigned a particular Church or definite people for the exercise of his power. When the *passive subject* of a power is lacking, the power, although it has been efficaciously conferred, lacks a determined flock to whom it is concretely directed. The coordination of the power of all the bishops is obtained by the fact that each bishop is assigned his own proper subjects so that there is no conflict with the exercise of the power of the rest of the bishops. The designation of people contributes an element that is necessary for the exercise of power. For this reason such designation has a causal aspect in rendering the exercise of power completely possible, while the adequate efficient cause of this is still episcopal consecration.

3. NECESSARY RECOGNITION OF A BISHOP ON THE PART OF THE ROMAN PONTIFF

There remains, therefore, the question of how recognition of the episcopal office is effected in the Church, i.e., how the exercise of episcopal power is coordinated with the exercise of power on the part of the rest of the bishops, how the consecrated bishop is incorporated within the Church's hierarchy of governing, and how communion is had with the rest of the bishops.

There can be no doubt that this recognition belongs to the Roman Pontiff in virtue of his primatial office. But if we maintain that this recognition belongs to the Roman Pontiff, we are not claiming that this recognition in every concrete case ought to be given directly by the Roman Pontiff himself. Rather we are saying that such recognition is not possible unless given either by the authority of the Roman Pontiff or in union with the authority of the Roman Pontiff.

Therefore, we can here prescind from the question of whether the Roman Pontiff enjoys power over the bishops inasmuch as he is the visible head of the universal Church, or inasmuch as he is the head of the college of bishops. The Roman Pontiff is, of course, the head of *the college*

63

of bishops. Hence it cannot be said that the coordination of the bishops' exercise of the power of governing is achieved through the college of bishops itself without the Roman Pontiff playing any part. For there is no college of bishops without the Roman Pontiff as its head. Hence the coordination of a bishop's exercise of power cannot be effected by the college of bishops without the Roman Pontiff. Furthermore, since the Roman Pontiff is the divinely constituted head of the college of bishops, his power is not constituted by the very college of bishops. The Roman Pontiff, therefore, would act as the head of the college of bishops in the name of the college of bishops, even if an explicit and formal mandate was not had from the college of bishops. He represents the college of bishops because of the power which is divinely constituted and conferred upon the subject of the primatial power.

On this supposition the power of recognizing a bishop belongs to the Roman Pontiff. For the point in question is the coordination of a consecrated bishop's exercise of his power of governing with the other bishops' exercise of their power of governing in the Church, and indeed in all issues of government. There must be, therefore, competence over the entire Church, every particular church, and every issue of government. Now the Roman Pontiff has *immediate, universal, episcopal* power,[17] namely, over the entire Church, every bishop, and every issue of government.

On the other hand the Roman Pontiff's episcopal power is not constituted as a substitute for the bishops' power of governing as this is divinely constituted and conferred upon a concrete subject through episcopal consecration.[18] Hence the Roman Pontiff's episcopal power is constituted for the coordination of the bishops' exercise of the power of governing.

64

This coordination consists principally in the fact that each bishop be given a determined part of the Church, a particular church or diocese, since the concrete division of the Church into particular churches is certainly not of divine law;[19] next, that common norms be established for all the bishops on the manner of exercising the power of governing in the concrete so that the common good of the Church may be established and preserved. The bishop, therefore, in obtaining recognition on the part of the Roman Pontiff obtains through such recognition a particular church and binds himself to the observance of the Church's common norms concerning the exercise of his power of governing. So actually his power of governing is coordinated with the power of governing of the other bishops for the sake of governing the Church and for the sake of settling issues. So actually it is for the sake of government that the bishop is in communion with the other bishops who exercise the power of governing in the Church and is thus received and incorporated within their college.

Such recognition of the episcopal office is therefore a major cause by its very nature, because it should stem at least mediately from the Roman Pontiff; the bishop's power of governing must at least be coordinated with the primatial power of governing. For there are many major causes of government which are such by their very nature (confer Can. 220). Hence, when there is no coordination of the bishop's exercise of the power of governing with the primatial power of governing, there is simply no coordination of the bishop's exercise of the power of governing with the exercise of the power of governing among others who are constituted in the Church by divine right to exercise the power of governing.[20]

In brief, therefore, it can and should be said: On the

65

one hand it is presupposed that the conferral of the episcopal office upon a concrete subject takes place by episcopal consecration; on the other hand it is presupposed that the primatial office with its inherent, true, episcopal power over the entire Church or over every particular church is of divine institution. Hence it is impossible for a concrete subject to possess a completely constituted episcopal office with the juridically efficacious exercise of the power of governing in the Church unless he is recognized by the Roman Pontiff. For, otherwise, the Roman Pontiff's episcopal power over the entire Church or in every particular church would be illusory. Accordingly, the concrete possibility of having a bishop who would not be recognized by the Roman Pontiff but would occupy the episcopal office in a juridically efficacious way would finally lead in its ultimate logic to the denial of the primatial power of the Roman Pontiff. A bishop cannot, therefore, be incorporated within the college of bishops who exercise the power of governing in the Church unless he is recognized by the Roman Pontiff. Hence the bishop's power of governing must be coordinated with the primatial power of governing. When this coordination is present, the coordination of the bishop's exercise of the power of governing with the exercise of the power of governing of the rest of the bishops is present; both incorporation in the college of bishops and communion with the other bishops for the sake of government are present.

Hence it follows that when the episcopal office has been sacramentally constituted (through valid episcopal consecration) but not recognized by the Roman Pontiff, an essential element is missing, namely, the *requisite* external structure in the Church that is required by divine law for the preservation of *the common good of the Church*, for the existence of unity between the head and members of the college of bishops, for the continued maintenance of the peace and tranquillity of the life of the Church, and for the efficacious establishment and conservation of communion in Christ and of the charity of Christ among the particular churches. Accordingly, the power of governing of a bishop who, although validly consecrated, is not recognized by the Roman Pontiff is not completely constituted and is, therefore, inefficacious. He does not have the exercise of the power of governing in the Church. It is true, furthermore, that he simply does not have any power of governing or jurisdiction. This bishop is simply not constituted to exercise the power of governing in the Church.

4. Various Juridical States of a Validly Consecrated Bishop

Under these suppositions, there are various juridical states possible for a bishop who has been divinely constituted (through valid episcopal consecration).

a) The bishop is validly constituted (through valid episcopal consecration). He has the episcopal office of divine right sacramentally conferred upon him; he has the substantially existent power of governing in the Church without any exercise of this power; he has jurisdiction substantially, but not efficaciously. According to Canon 348 § 1 this status is lawful in a *Titular Bishop* who is validly consecrated with the requisite authorization of the Roman Pontiff. This status is unlawful in a bishop who is validly consecrated, but without the requisite authorization of the Roman Pontiff.

b) A consecrated bishop receives a *canonical mission* in accordance with Canon 109 or a *canonical investiture* in accordance with Canon 332 § 1. He thus obtains the exercise of the power of governing in the Church which was conferred through episcopal consecration; he receives jurisdiction to be exercised in a diocese. He also receives juridiction to be exercised over the universal Church in an Ecumenical Council (either antecedently or consequently to jurisdiction in a diocese [cf. note 15 supra]). For since the bishop has received the recognition of his power of governing in the Church from the Roman Pontiff, the essential condition of divine law—inasmuch as the recognition of a bishop on the part of the Roman Pontiff is a major cause of its very nature—has been fulfilled for the attainment of the exercise of the power of governing in the Church which had been substantially conferred through episcopal consecration, i.e., for the efficacious possession of jurisdiction.

The Roman Pontiff in granting canonical investiture is truly a cause, from which the efficacious jurisdiction of the bishop is immediately derived, because he bestows upon the bishop an element that is essential and necessary for the possession of *efficacious* jurisdiction. For the Roman Pontiff in granting recognition to the bishop brings about the coordination of the bishop's power of governing with the power of governing of the rest of the bishops in the Church. It is due, moreover, to this coordination that the external structure of the bishop's power of governing can be formed since the efficient cause of this power (namely episcopal consecration) is made efficacious in relation to the creation of the external structure of the power of governing. Accordingly the recognition of a bishop on the part of the Roman Pontiff makes possible the formation of an essential element that is necessary for the efficacious possession of the power of governing in the Church. In-

68

deed, this coordination through the Roman Pontiff is accomplished by the fact that a particular church or a determined people are bestowed upon the bishop for the exercise of his power of governing in the Church. For this reason, therefore, the element necessary to render fully possible the exercise of the power conferred through episcopal consecration is contributed by the Roman Pontiff. That is to say, the *passive subject* of this power is constituted. For this reason, therefore, it truly must be said that the recognition of the bishop on the part of the Roman Pontiff constitutes the cause from which the bishop's exercise of jurisdiction is immediately derived.[21]

c) A bishop is forbidden the exercise of his jurisdiction either as a penalty—excommunication (Can. 2264) or suspension (Can. 2284)—or simply by losing office inasmuch as it is a canonical office (Can. 183 ff.). Insofar as the prohibition of the exercise of jurisdiction does not affect the validity of the actions of jurisdiction but merely their liceity, there is no necessity for discussion of this in the present context. Insofar, however, as the prohibition affects the validity of the acts of jurisdiction, the bishop cannot lose the episcopal office itself, since it is conferred through episcopal consecration. In other words he cannot lose the very power of governing in the Church in its substance, just as the baptized cannot lose the fundamental rights of the supernatural order which were constituted in their substance by valid baptism itself. He does lose, however, all exercise of the sacramentally conferred power of governing in the Church, so that such exercise, when unlawfully attempted, lacks all efficacy juridically and is, consequently, invalid. The juridical status of such a bishop is the juridical status of a consecrated bishop without any efficacious jurisdiction. And we have just stated that such a status can be lawful or unlawful. It is lawful, for example, in the case of a residential bishop who has renounced his (canonical) office and is then ordinarily designated a titular bishop.

Under these suppositions, moreover, a good explanation is also afforded of the *reservation of a particular cause* by the Holy See. If it is a question of a cause for which the bishop of himself by divine right would have competence (i.e., for which the power is sacramentally conferred in its substance by episcopal consecration), the reservation of the cause, either in a particular instance or in general, suspends for the common good of the Church the juridically efficacious exercise of the bishop's or bishops' power of governing. For the Roman Pontiff is obliged to look out for the common good of the Church, and this can demand the suspension of the exercise of a power in the consideration of concrete circumstances in different parts of the Church.

5. FACULTIES CONSTITUTING THE EPISCOPAL OFFICE BY DIVINE LAW

If, then, one asks what sort of faculties are included in the divinely constituted and sacramentally conferred power of governing of the bishop, it seems that the reply must be: this power of governing includes the faculties that are required for government in the Church and, in particular, for the government of a particular church under ordinary circumstances. For the episcopal office was by divine law constituted for this purpose. The question, however, of whether this or that particular power constitutes an essential part of the episcopal office or not, is of minor practical importance since the exercise of the episcopal office must be completely coordinated with the exercise of the primatial office. Hence, as we have just said, there can be considerations deriving from the common good of the universal Church that demand that some specific cause be decided by the supreme power. In this supposition there is a *major cause of positive law* (Can. 220).

Thus, for example, in accordance with the norm of Canon 1257, "it is the function of the one Holy See both to determine liturgy and to approve liturgical books." Supposing that we are dealing with a major cause by positive law, not one by its very nature (we can prescind from this question here), this reservation is explained by the fact that in the Church's actual condition its common good demands that this cause be decided by the Holy See.[22]

Similarly, supposing the opinion that the faculty of dispensing from vows belongs of itself to the bishops, the reservation of some vows is explained by the fact that the common good of the Church demands that the dispensation from vows that are reserved in accordance with Canon 1309 be made by the Holy See. This would be, therefore, a major cause by positive law.[23]

In either case, therefore, the bishops in virtue of their divinely constituted and sacramentally conferred power of governing in the Church would have power in substance and existence over these causes but by positive law they would not have the exercise of this power. Consequently, the exercise of their power in these causes would be juridically inefficacious or simply invalid.[24]

6. COLLEGIATE EXERCISE OF THE EPISCOPAL OFFICE OF GOVERNING IN THE CHURCH

A bishop who is recognized by the Roman Pontiff is incorporated by such recognition within the college of

71

bishops, whose head is the Roman Pontiff himself. Hence the bishops are in communion with him and with one another. The efficacious jurisdiction proper to bishops is possessed not only over the particular Church entrusted to the individual bishops, but also in the collegiate administration of the universal Church along with the rest of the bishops, inasmuch as they are to be summoned to an *Ecumenical Council* and have the right of deliberative vote (Can. 223 § 1, 1). The possession of the exercise of the power of governing the Church collegiately is to be explained in the same way as we did the exercise of this power in the diocese: the power is conferred in its substance in episcopal consecration, but is rendered efficacious through recognition on the part of the Roman Pontiff. This recognition incorporates the bishop within the college of bishops for the exercise of the power of governing in the Church collegiately along with the rest of the bishops.

Moreover, in precisely the same way a solution is also presented to that much debated question of the nature of the power exercised by titular bishops in an Ecumenical Council. For titular bishops "when summoned to the Council have a deliberative vote unless other provision is expressly made in the decree of convocation" (Can. 223 § 2). Certainly they have no efficacious jurisdiction over a particular church of themselves, because (in keeping with the law) their power of governing is not coordinated with the rest of the bishops. But this non-coordination of the power of governing is restricted to the power of governing a particular church. The power of governing that is ordained to the universal Church is exercised to its highest degree principally in an Ecumenical Council. Nothing, therefore, prevents the titular bishops' power of governing, which was sacramentally conferred in its substance in episcopal consecration, from becoming efficacious in an Ecumenical Council although it is not efficacious in any particular church. In other words, the Roman Pontiff coordinates the titular bishops with the rest of the bishops in the exercise of power in an Ecumenical Council; thus even the titular bishops, if present at the Council, exercise the office which was divinely constituted and sacramentally conferred in its substance and existence, and recognized with relation to the Ecumenical Council by the Roman Pontiff, so that it can be efficaciously exercised in the Council. Accordingly, the exercise of universal jurisdiction in the sense just explained, which residential bishops acquire by canonical investiture itself, is acquired by titular bishops with respect to the Council if they are summoned to it.

The other ways of exercising the power of governing in the Church collegiately under current legislation (*The Code of Canon Law*) are *Plenary Councils and Provincial Councils* (Can. 281–292). There is almost no need to mention that the power which the bishops collegiately exercise in such Councils is substantially conferred in episcopal consecration and becomes efficacious upon recognition of the bishops on the part of the Roman Pontiff, and by observance of the norms which have been established for these Councils by the supreme authority of the Church. The same remarks that were made with respect to an Ecumenical Council are to be applied to the exercise of the power of titular bishops in these Councils. For titular bishops, who have been legitimately summoned to them, have a deliberative vote in plenary and provincial councils (Can. 282 § 1; 286 § 2).

Conferences of Bishops in accordance with the norm of Canon 292 are made up of the local Ordinaries of an ecclesiastical Province. There are scarcely any norms of common law for such conferences. Nonetheless, in recent decades they have acquired an ever increasing importance for ecclesiastical life; they are not restricted to bishops of an ecclesiastical province, but are rather extended to the bishops of an entire territory. It should be noted, however, that the statutes of these conferences are obliging only to the extent to which they are promulgated in the individual diocese by the Local Ordinary himself. For a conference of bishops has no jurisdiction in a province or territory.

Doubtless the development of social life in our times can demand some canonical prescriptions as suitable or necessary for an entire territory. Actually in the meetings of the first session of the Second Vatican Council such conferences of bishops were frequently discussed. The Fathers especially expressed the wish that conferences of bishops have the faculty of establishing particular territorial legislation in those matters which preclude or make inopportune a universal solution.

In principle there seems to be no obstacle to granting such faculties to conferences of bishops. On this supposition, the exercise of power in conferences of bishops is to be explained just as it was in the question of plenary and provincial councils which such conferences closely resemble in their constitution. It should be noted, however, that on this supposition also the statutes of the conference of bishops are truly binding on the complete territory and that the promulgation of such statutes in his own diocese is not left to the discretion of the individual bishop.[25]

74

7. EPISCOPAL OFFICE OF PATRIARCH, PRIMATE, AND METROPOLITAN

In the Latin Church under current legislation (Can. 271) Patriarchs and Primates as such do not have jurisdiction. The Metropolitan or Archbishop has those faculties which are exhaustively listed in Canon 274. In the Oriental Church, on the contrary, the Patriarch has true jurisdiction.[26] The questions which arise from this point do not require treatment here. The sole object of our enquiry is an explanation of the power of governing of such a prelate who possesses as the passive subject of his power many particular churches, and hence the bishops who are in charge of such dioceses.

Concerning the power in particular which the *Oriental Patriarch* possesses, it is doubtless the result of historical development and thus truly founded on ancient tradition. There is no doubt that the Holy See gives the utmost reverence and recognition to the power founded on such a tradition. Nevertheless, the metaphysical structure of this power is not different from any other such episcopal power of governing in the Church. Here also we are dealing with the sacramentally conferred power (through episcopal consecration) of governing in the Church which *by the recognition of the Roman Pontiff* is coordinated in its exercise with the right to govern of the rest of the bishops, not only for the sake of government in the Patriarch's own diocese but also, within the limits of law, for the sake of patriarchal government over the entire territory of the patriarchate, its bishops and faithful. Hence it seems to us that all further questions are for this reason of minor importance, as, for example, whether this power is a

75

privilege, or does the historical evolution of power constitute of itself a juridical title to patriarchal power.[27] For whatever may be decided in such issues, any solution must finally be reduced to the ultimate basis, i.e., this power is possessed in its substance by episcopal consecration and in its efficacy by the recognition which the Patriarch as such receives from the Roman Pontiff.

No further explanation, therefore, is required for the fact that the power of the Metropolitan has the same structure. This is true of any prelate who has been consecrated a bishop to exercise the power of governing, thus conferred upon him, over many dioceses. Moreover, there does not seem to be any difficulty in itself in the fact that a prelate who has been consecrated a bishop is appointed a bishop to govern a particular group of the faithful, as is occasionally the actual practice among the faithful of the Oriental rites who live in Latin lands.

8. Solutions to Difficulties

The historical origin of the intervention of the Roman Pontiff in the investiture of bishops

A possible objection to the explanation proposed in these pages is that it is impossible to speak of the Roman Pontiff's intervention in the investiture of bishops for many centuries. This fact is, of course, not to be denied. But we cannot conclude that it contradicts the assertion that the investiture of a bishop is a major cause by its very nature, especially because of the necessary coordination of the bishop's power of governing with the power of governing of the rest of the bishops and with the primatial power of the Roman Pontiff.

First of all we must declare that the Church has always demanded legitimate *recognition of a bishop* according to the practice of the times.[28] Thus it is certain that in the first centuries the Church conferred the power of governing through the imposition of hands. This imposition of hands, however, was of itself of no avail for the legitimate exercise of the power received. Rather, for this the incorporation of the bishop within the Church's hierarchy of governing, the coordination of the bishop with the rest of the bishops, was also necessary. An unrecognized bishop could not legitimately exercise his power of governing.[29] The lawful process for such recognition in the first centuries was es- tablished by tradition or *custom*, to which, as such, the First Council of Nicaea had already appealed..[30] The First Council of Nicaea itself established a *law*[31] on this matter. Hence the mode of such recognition (that is by the bishops and Metropolitan of an ecclesiastical province) was con- firmed by the supreme ecclesiastical authority which is non-existent without the Roman Pontiff.

But the more the Church expanded, and her life de- veloped and actively influenced the entire social life, and the more that secular rulers sought to influence the ap- pointment of bishops, the more necessary became the intervention of the primatial office for the coordination of all those who exercise government in the Church. The very vicissitudes that the creation of bishops experienced in the Middle Ages, which were frequently denounced and attacked by the Roman Pontiffs as contrary to canonical prescription, prove the necessity of such intervention on the part of the Roman Pontiff for the common good of the Church and for the defence of the independence of the Church's government from secular power.[32]

77

Consequently the non-exercise of the prerogative of the primatial office in this matter does not prove that this very primatial prerogative did not exist. Such non-exercise of this prerogative should not even be explained as a tacit concession made to others (for example, to the bishops of an ecclesiastical province). Rather, the condition of the Church in the first centuries simply did not demand the intervention of the Roman Pontiff. Later the condition of the Church utterly demanded this intervention. In this sense historical development did not create this prerogative of the primatial office, but rather revealed it.

These, then, are the facts: a bishop who had been canonically and lawfully constituted (in accordance with the norms prevailing at that time, namely, through episcopal consecration for a determined, particular church), acquired the power of governing in the Church not only in its substance and existence, but also with consecration he acquired the efficacious power of governing since with lawful recognition the external structure of episcopal power was formed. For a bishop is constituted to govern in the Church. Therefore, a bishop who was thus promoted also had the exercise of his power of governing. But once the necessity of the intervention of the Roman Pontiff has been established for the bishop's possession of a canonical mission to a particular Church, the lack of this intervention or recognition renders the bishop's power of governing juridically inefficacious. For such power lacks the external structure lawfully required in the Church and further established by divine law since episcopal power must be coordinated with the primatial power of the Roman Pontiff. Hence episcopal power cannot be exercised as long as there continues to be a lack of recognition of the episcopal office on the part of the Roman Pontiff. In this case there is a *subjective* dogmatic growth which was necessitated by the development of the life of the Church.[33]

The separability of the power of jurisdiction from the sacramental conferral of the episcopal office

A further difficulty could be found in that through episcopal consecration power of jurisdiction is not truly conferred, but "a person is constituted in the degrees of jurisdiction by a canonical mission" (Can. 109). This difficulty can be further pressed by the fact that primatial or episcopal power of jurisdiction can be present even in a subject who has not yet been consecrated a bishop. Furthermore, the power of jurisdiction can in turn be taken even from a consecrated bishop, while the power of orders, once obtained through episcopal consecration, cannot be lost.

It could be said that this difficulty does not directly affect our principal assertion, namely, that the episcopal office, divinely conferred upon a subject, does not suffice for the exercise of this office. To exercise this office, recognition on the part of the Roman Pontiff is necessary. Moreover we can prescind from the precise way in which the office is divinely conferred.[34]

Nevertheless, there is actually hardly any question of the fact that the imposition of hands or episcopal consecration plays an essential part in the bestowal of the divinely conferred episcopal power. Hence the episcopal office is sacramentally conferred. And so, granted the opinion that the episcopal office is divinely conferred through episcopal consecration, the aforementioned difficulty can truly be solved. For the fact that the jurisdiction of the Roman Pontiff and of the bishop can be possessed antecedently to episcopal consecration needs some explanation.

1. Under existing legislation a bishop-elect is certainly constituted *bishop* of a particular Church by the canonical investiture which is given by the Roman Pontiff (Can. 332 § 1). On the other hand he has no title to the valid exercise of power in a diocese before canonically taking possession of it (Can. 334 § 2). Ordinarily, therefore, episcopal consecration, which the bishop-elect is absolutely required to receive within three months from the reception of the apostolic letters, takes place between canonical investiture and canonical possession. Consequently, possession of the diocese should occur within four months from investiture (Can. 333). Accordingly, the very power of the bishop-elect in his diocese, antecedent to his episcopal consecration and act of possession, is a theoretical rather than a practical issue. For this reason as well, under existing legislation, the power of governing is of no practical importance in a subject who has not yet been consecrated a bishop. Accordingly, in this sense from apostolic times it has been the constant practice of the Church that those who exercise the episcopal power of governing have previously received the imposition of hands.[35] Furthermore absolute episcopal ordination was explicitly prohibited for centuries so that an individual who was consecrated absolutely had no exercise of the power received, and if he attempted to exercise it, it would have been invalid at least in regard to the power of governing.[36] Thus it is clear that the Church at that time, i.e., during the entire first millennium, did not consider the episcopal power of governing present in a subject not yet consecrated a bishop.

Although under existing legislation a bishop-elect may therefore have jurisdiction antecedent to episcopal consecration, it must be maintained that such a condition is not absolute nor the rule. For actually since the episcopal office is an office of divine right to be sacramentally conferred upon a subject, it is not completely constituted before episcopal consecration. Hence *the metaphysical structure* of the divinely constituted office that is to be sacramentally conferred on a subject cannot be derived from such a condition which is truly accidental.

Moreover, it can be maintained that jurisdiction over a diocese, which is perhaps present in the subject before episcopal consecration, is certainly truly possessed for the government of the diocese. Whereas the episcopal power of governing, since it is divinely constituted as a single and complete reality that also contains the power of orders, and must therefore be sacramentally conferred on a subject, still lacks its ontological fundament, i.e., the sacramental or episcopal character in which it inheres; it consequently lacks its "substratum," namely, its very substance which must be sacramentally conferred. The bishop therefore truly acquires his position in the hierarchy of jurisdiction by the canonical mission. The canonical mission, however, of itself ordinarily renders efficacious the power of governing that has been sacramentally conferred in its substance and existence.

Furthermore, it must be noted that the current practice is a precise continuation of the ancient custom in episcopal ordination, for even now a bishop is always consecrated with a title to a particular church, although perhaps this church has already been extinct for centuries in the case of titular bishops. Hence it is clear that the Church has

81

always maintained and still maintains that the episcopal office must be divinely conferred upon a concrete subject through episcopal consecration.

2. As to the primatial power of the Roman Pontiff: when a candidate is canonically elected with manifest consent, "he is true Pope, and actually acquires and can exercise full and absolute jurisdiction over the entire world."[37] There is no need to discuss in this context questions concerned with the acquisition of primatial power. It can, however, be remarked here that this statement is not in opposition to the proposed opinion that episcopal power is sacramentally conferred in its substance through episcopal consecration.

Truly, "the Roman Pontiff, when lawfully elected, immediately upon acceptance of his election, has by divine right full power of supreme jurisdiction" (Can. 219). But there is an immediate addition "if the man chosen is not yet a priest or bishop . . . he shall be ordained and consecrated."[38] Therefore, under existing legislation the unity of the Supreme Pontiff's episcopal power is also shown because it has a fundament which must be sacramentally conferred. Thus if we prescind from the fact that the Pontiff-elect in our time generally is a Bishop already, in the case of the Roman Pontiff, too, the primatial power before reception of episcopal consecration is a thing of no great practical significance.

As a matter of fact, in antiquity, because of the sacramental fundament which is necessary for the Roman Pontiff's power of governing, the creation of the Supreme Pontiff was looked upon as the creation of a bishop. Since ordinations were always performed for a determined particular church, during almost the entire first millennium translations of bishops hardly ever occurred.[39] Consequently, when elected, the Roman Pontiffs were generally clerics (less than bishops) of the Roman church, or merely deacons.[40] Certainly, therefore, primatial power of jurisdiction was possessed by means of canonical election and acceptance. Nonetheless the very creation of a Supreme Pontiff was considered perfect only with episcopal consecration.[41] Hence in the case of the Roman Pontiff the Church did not consider the power of governing completely constituted in a subject not yet consecrated a bishop.[42]

Finally, with the recognition in the Church of the reflex distinction between the power of orders and the power of jurisdiction all human causality was excluded from the origin of the primatial power of jurisdiction. In particular, therefore, the causality of divine activity which, as mediated through the Roman Pontiff, is held to be the source of the bishops' power of jurisdiction, had to be considered the immediate source of the primatial power. A bishop needs incorporation within the college of bishops and coordination of the exercise of his power of governing through the Roman Pontiff; the Roman Pontiff, the head of the college of bishops, is constituted by God Himself from whom he receives the government of the entire Church.[43]

And so, although under existing legislation primatial jurisdiction can be present in the Pontiff-elect antecedent to episcopal consecration, it must be said that this condition is not natural nor the rule. For actually the primatial office of the Sovereign Pontiff, since it is an office of divine right to be sacramentally conferred on a subject, is not completely constituted before episcopal consecration. Hence, the metaphysical structure of the perfectly constituted primatial office cannot be derived from such a condition which is truly accidental.

83

Accordingly the canonical Pontiff-elect is truly constituted the head of the Church and of all the bishops and faithful by his very election and acceptance, so that by such divine constitution he receives the government of the entire Church. Hence in the constitution of the head of the hierarchy of the Church there is no human causality, so that on the highest level of hierarchy the subject is immediately constituted by God Himself along with acceptance of canonical election.[44] Yet since the primatial power constitutes a single complete entity with the power of orders because it is truly episcopal power inherent in a sacramental fundament, it manifestly lacks its ontological (namely the sacramental) fundament before episcopal consecration, i.e., it lacks its "substratum," or the sacramental constitution of its substance. Consequently, primatial power is not perfect before consecration, as is already clear from the fact that antecedent to consecration the Pontiff-elect could grant jurisdiction for sacramental absolution but could not himself sacramentally absolve— at least if he were as yet only a deacon. Accordingly, the primatial office of the Supreme Pontiff, the Bishop of the church of Rome and of the entire Church, is perfectly constituted as soon as there is a canonical election and acceptance together with episcopal consecration of the subject.

CONCLUSIONS

The concept of the metaphysical structure of the episcopal office that has been proposed in these pages preserves and explains the necessary elements and simultaneously brings out the sacramental foundation and the christological and ecclesiological nature of all the power in the Church.

1. On the one hand the principle that the episcopal office is of divine right and is divinely conferred on a concrete subject has to be preserved. On the other hand the principle that the primatial power is truly episcopal power over the entire Church and all pastors has to be preserved. Hence investiture of bishops is impossible independently of the Supreme Pontiff. Moreover, the possibility of the juridical influence of the Roman Pontiff upon the exercise of the bishops' power of ruling, either in a particular case or through general precept, is necessary for the preservation of Church unity, for the preservation of unity of government, and for the establishment and conservation of the common good of the universal Church. These aspects are preserved by the fact that the very *episcopal office* is actually divinely conferred upon a concrete subject through episcopal consecration; in other words the power of governing in the Church is *sacramentally* constituted in its substance and existence in a concrete subject. The exercise, however, of the power of ruling or *efficacious jurisdiction* is not therefore already present in the bishop, as long as he lacks recognition by the Roman Pontiff, canonical investiture on the part of the Roman Pontiff.

2. An explanation is needed of how the episcopal office with its inherent power of governing in the Church can be divinely conferred, namely, through episcopal consecration, without the valid exercise of the power of governing which was thus conferred. A distinction that follows with metaphysical necessity between the internal and external structures of human sociability, even when supernaturally elevated, affords the solution to this difficulty. *The power of governing in the Church in its substance* is related to the internal structure of supernaturally elevated human sociability. This internal structure of super-

naturally elevated human sociability is the result of a sacramental activity, the vicarious activity of Christ the Lord, so that it is constituted rationally antecedent to the Church as a human society and cannot be affected by it. Actually the episcopal power of governing in the Church in its substance, in its ontological substratum, its intentional being, is the result of sacramental activity, namely episcopal consecration; this power is based upon the character of the episcopal order in which it inheres.

This sacramentally conferred power is, however, ordered to the Church as the human society in which it must be exercised. Accordingly *the exercise of this power* requires coordination with the exercise of the power of governing of the rest of the bishops in the Church; it requires incorporation within the Church's hierarchy of government. If this incorporation is wanting, the power of governing in the Church lacks an essential element, namely, the requisite external structure, so that it is not completely constituted and cannot be exercised; the episcopal office is not juridically and efficaciously possessed or simply is not possessed.

Incorporation of the bishop within the hierarchy of the Church, within the college of bishops, must be accomplished through *canonical investiture on the part of the Roman Pontiff*, because the primatial power has been established by Christ the Lord as the basis of unity of government in the Church to coordinate the exercise of the power of governing on the part of every bishop in the entire Church.

This conception is confirmed by the historical development of the conferral of the episcopal office. For what has always been considered necessary is not only episcopal consecration but at the same time recognition of the conse-

20:28) permits no alternative such as the following: the episcopal power of governing in the Church is the product of either episcopal consecration or the Roman Pontiff. Rather the episcopal office with its inherent power of governing in the Church is the result of both episcopal consecration and the canonical mission on the part of the Roman Pontiff. The episcopal office is derived both from Christ the Lord so that in such an office the mission of the Apostles, which proceeded from the Lord and has been constantly sacramentally entrusted anew by this very Lord, endures to the consummation of the world; and from the recognition of the consecrated bishop on the part of the Roman Pontiff, the Vicar of Christ, so that the exercise of the power of governing is truly possessed in communion with all of the bishops in the Church and can be the source of peace. Accordingly the origin, nature, and conferral of the episcopal office, since it must be reduced to Christ the Lord, together with its ordination to the Church, because the episcopal office has been constituted "for the building up of the Body of Christ—which is the Church—in love" (Eph. 4:16; Col. 1:24) are as apparent as possible.

Notes

1. Willibald M. Plöchl, Geschichte des Kirchenrechts, I (Wien-München, 1953), 205 and 361; II (1955), 264 f.

2. Acts 20:17; 1 Tim. 1:3; 3:1 ff.; 5:22; Tit. 1:5–9; 1 Pet 5:1. "The age of the apostolic Fathers is an age of transition. This is most clearly manifested by the fact that in this period the Church's itinerant missionaries more and more disappear. They had first of all replaced the Apostles in whose company many of them had begun their apostolate. As Timothy and Titus, so others may have already received from an Apostle a commission that was limited to one place" (Matthäus Kaiser, Die Einheit der Kirchengewalt nach dem Zeugnis des Neuen Testamentes und der Apostolischen Väter [München, 1956], pp. 191 f.).

3. "Absolute ordination, i.e., clerical consecration without a binding tie to a specific ecclesiastical institution, is encountered from the middle of the fourth century on in the West as well as in the East. . . . The origin and blossoming of this practice are intimately, but certainly not exclusively, connected with monasticism. . . . Absolute ordinations cannot be traced back earlier than the fourth century. But the presumption is not unfounded that they did not first arise at that time, but that, as the remains of the early missionary order, they never completely died out" (Vinzenz Fuchs, *Der Ordinationstitel von seiner Entstehung bis auf Innozenz III* [Bonn, 1930] Kanonistische Studien und Texte, IV, 103, with n. 2).

4. "The holy synod decreed that the imposition of hands upon those who are absolutely ordained is void, and to the disgrace of him who performed the ordination, the actions of such men have no validity" (The Council of Chalcedon (451), Can. 6 in *Gratiani Decretum*, p. I, dist. 70, c. 1 [ed. Friedberg I], 257). "The Council of Chalcedon, which represents a definite conclusion to the development of canon law in the Roman Empire and a summary of previous legislation, earnestly sought to guarantee the organization of the diocese and in particular subordination to the bishop. . . . Absolute ordination stood in sharp contrast to this indispensable structure of the ecclesiastical order. . . . The absolutely ordained individual was a foreign-body in the organic cell structure of the ecclesiastical order" (Fuchs, *op. cit.*, IV, 123 f.).

5. Plöchl, *op. cit.*, II, 264 f.

6. "But although our predecessors would have wished that the ordinations of those promoted to orders without a definite title be null and void to the disgrace of those performing the ordinations, we, however, desiring to be more indulgent wish that the ordinees be cared for by the ordainers and their successors until they acquire ecclesiastical benefices through them" (C. 16, lib. extra, de praebendis et dignitatibus, III, 5 [ed. Friedberg II], 469). Concerning Innocence III's mandate Fuchs remarks: "Innocence's action really prepared the way for the complete conquest of the old legislation on ordination; for the complete separation of consecration and investiture; for the legal recognition of absolute ordination" (*Op. cit.*, pp. 274 f.).

7. On the doctrinal development of this point in the Middle Ages till the time of the decretists cf. Fuchs, *op. cit.*, Part IV.

8. "God bestows the grace of office through human hands. Both elements are equally significant: the divinely conferred gift and the mediation through man. It is precisely this latter aspect that should not be underestimated. Of course, it is God Himself who invites the candidate for office with the spiritual and efficacious endowments; but God makes use of mediation through a visible process, the imposition of hands.

"It is not just the mere imposition of hands but rather the imposition of hands of one authorized to do so that permits the power of God to flow to men. It is not a question of a mechanical transmission of what the person himself possesses. Doubtless the candidate for office does become endowed with the same competence as the person who imposes hands on him possesses, but not because this competence flows from one to the other. Rather it is because this competence, while mediated by the imposition of hands of the consecrator, is bestowed by God in the same way as the consecrator also received it. Thus, the ecclesiastical official always remains, throughout the ages, in the same proximity to the divine source of all ecclesiastical power. In this way the mission given by the Lord to the Apostles remains alive in the Church: in the constant repetition of this mission by our exalted Lord under the sign of the imposition of hands of His authorized vicars, as well as in the fulfilment of this mission by the individual officials in the Church" (Kaiser, op. cit., p. 116 f.).

9. "The prayer added to the imposition of hands makes it clear that the Lord Himself is working concealed within this action. While the Apostles received their power directly from the Lord, after them the successors of the Apostles are given their power by the Lord through the mediation of the Apostles in the imposition of hands. Therefore, a confrontation with Christ takes place in this instance also. Although it is not an immediate confrontation, it is nonetheless a confrontation in the sacramental sign.

"The inadmissibility and the concomitant non-reiterability of the act of communication are based upon this communication of power by the Lord, even if it is mediate. But its legal character is based upon the mediation through human hands" (Kaiser, op. cit., pp. 121 f.). "According to his various functions, the successor of the Apostles uses his power in its priestly, teaching or governing aspect. But this fact tells us nothing definite about the internal nature of ecclesiastical power. In all circumstances this nature is one and the same. It cannot be defined by its duties, but only by the mission by the Lord.

"The ecclesiastical mission was realized by men, by the Apostles or their delegates. This involves the mediation of a gift of God. The successors of the Apostles are endowed with the Holy Ghost. Consequently, their power is ultimately divine not only in its origin but also in its nature. Therein lies the foundation of its substantial unit. The statement, that the successors of the Apostles exercise not a human but a divine power makes it clear that we are not dealing with several, essential and naturally distinct powers but with a single power, as befits the divine nature, which can become effective in various functions" (Kaiser, op. cit., p. 137). "As Christ is sent by the Father, so the Apostles and all further (future) successors of the Apostles are sent by the Lord. This mission remains vital in the Church. Since it is given to the individual successors of the Apostles not for their own sakes but with a view to the Church, we refer to it simply as the power of the Church; this, as such, has a legal character and its peculiarity consists in this fact, that men vis-à-vis the entire Church or a part thereof authoritatively represent Jesus Christ. This legal character includes the Church's power as such in its unity and entirety; it also includes the relationship of representation of Christ. Jesus Christ entrusted the word and the sacraments to the Apostles and thus placed these in the hands of the Church. For this reason—there are others which we can prescind from now—the institution of chorepiscopi was attacked and finally suppressed. In the East it disappeared in the eighth century. In the West, where it especially flourished in the eighth and ninth centuries, it was thereafter suppressed also. On these questions confer: Fuchs, *op. cit.*, IV, 130–137, 195–236; Plöchl, *op. cit.*, I, 53 f., 301 ff.

11. The few episcopal translations that are attested, e.g., St. Gregory Nazianzen, are explained by extraordinary circumstances so that such exceptions confirm the rule of non-translation. Cf. Fuchs, *op. cit.*, IV, 78–90.

12. On this point confer the citations in the previous notes from Kaiser and Fuchs. Episcopal consecration is intrinsically the consecration of a subject who is constituted to govern. "Grant him, O Lord, the episcopal chair to govern Thy Church and Thy people who are entrusted to him. Be Thou his authority; be Thou his power; be Thou his strength" (*Pontificale Romanum*, De consecratione Electi in Episcopum). And at present in the Oriental Church "upon reception of episcopal ordination the bishop . . . acquires episcopal jurisdiction." ("De personis physicis et moralibus," Can. 396 § 2, 1. *Acta Apostolicae Sedis* 49 [1957], 550.) "Finally, we must say that the episcopal dignity has been designated by divine law for the ordinary power of governing . . . namely, insofar as the divine law bids that the Church . . . be governed by means of bishops" (Ludovicus Billot, *De Ecclesiae Sacramentis*, tomus posterior [Romae, 1929[7]], 311 f.). "But the essence *iuris divini* (of the Episcopacy) cannot logically be sought only in those powers alone which are called the episcopal *potestas ordinis*. . . . The *ius divinum* which must be, and certainly is, part of the essence of the episcopacy will have to be sought for and especially in the *potestas iurisdictionis*" (Karl Rahner, *Episkopat und Primat* [Freiburg-Basel-Wien, 1961], pp. 65 f.).

13. "If the mission given by the Lord includes the command to pass on their power, the *method* of this transferral is not determined in detail by the Lord. There is nothing on this subject in the New-Testament sources. Therefore, we must make the following distinction: the *command* which the Apostles received from the Lord is always the same; it necessarily implies that the Apostles pass on their power. But *the method of this transferral* is not mentioned in the command itself. It is up to the Apostles to develop a form that is suitable for it. That the Apostles, in fulfillment of this task, seized upon an institution of Jewish law (namely, *impositio manuum*) is not surprising. As members of the Jewish people they were familiar with the practices of the juridico-religious life of this people. Thus, as a matter of course, they took over concepts, forms, and institutions from the pre-christian Jewish legal tradition" (Kaiser, *op. cit.*, p. 120).

14. We here understand the power of Christ as His power as *the mediator between God and men* with no further distinction as to whether this power belongs to Christ as priest, prophet, and king. Consequently, we also understand the fulness of the priesthood to be the fulness of power

transmitted to the Church which also contains the power of Christ as king and prophet.

Therefore, the Church's power is for this reason the vicarious power of Christ. This power, moreover, is given to the Church as her very own. Consequently, it is here not merely understood as that power which is called in a technical sense the vicarious power of Christ. Nor are we dealing in this context with the question of whether the power of teaching and the power of governing are adequately distinct. But we presuppose that the power of teaching and governing make up the Church's power of jurisdiction, generically considered. For this opinion—very ancient and by far the more common opinion today—results from the fact that the teaching of Christ constitutes divine revelation and is, therefore, of its very nature authoritative whether it is demanding faith or a life conformed to the teaching which is being preached. The Church has so conceived her power from the very beginning. Cf. *supra*, n. 9.

15. We are here prescinding from the question of whether a bishop is *directly and immediately* constituted for a particular church and, therefore, is a member of the college of bishops consequent to this constitution for a particular church, or whether he is rather directly and immediately constituted a member of the college of bishops and consequently acquires the government of a particular church because he is a member of the college of bishops. K. Rahner, S.J., defends the latter thesis: "Jesus established a college. Within it the individuals have power precisely insofar as and only insofar as they are members of this college" (*Op. cit.*, p. 71). "The college of bishops as such exists as the supreme bearer of the entire Church's authoritative power prior to the individual bishop as such. The bishop is first of all a member of the entire episcopacy as the collegiate governing agent of the Church which has in the Pope *iure divino* its abiding unity and the possibility of lasting concrete activity" (*Ibid.*, pp. 80 f.).

16. Cf. Part I of this study. Furthermore, episcopal power which has been sacramentally conferred, but not recognized by the Church, cannot be considered inefficacious because its efficient causality is nullified by the Church. For validly received episcopal consecration always produces the episcopal character in which episcopal power inheres. Hence episcopal power which has been substantially conferred through episcopal consecration is necessarily rendered inefficacious by blocking the formation of its external structure. When this essential element is lacking, episcopal power is not completely constituted. Cf. *supra*, Part I, note 42.

17. "We teach . . . that this power of jurisdiction of the Roman Pontiff, which is truly episcopal, is immediate: and that pastors as well as the faithful of every rite and dignity, both individually and as a body, are obliged to hierarchical subordination and true obedience to it, not only in affairs which pertain to faith and morals but also in affairs that are concerned with the discipline and government of the Church that is spread throughout the entire world; so that, in the preservation of the unity, both

of one communion and of the profession of the same faith with the Roman Pontiff, the Church of Christ may be one flock under one supreme shepherd" (*Concilium Vaticanum I, Constitutio dogmatica I de Ecclesia Christi*, Cap. 3, Denzinger-Schönmetzer, 3010 [1827]).

18. "But so far is this power of the Supreme Pontiff from interfering with that ordinary and immediate power of episcopal jurisdiction, by which the bishops, 'by appointment of the Holy Ghost' the successors of the Apostles, as true shepherds tend and govern the individual flocks entrusted to each of them, that this same power of episcopal jurisdiction is defended, strengthened and protected by the supreme and universal shepherd" (*Ibid.*, 3061 [1828]).

19. The power of governing which is substantially conferred by episcopal consecration has no determined *passive subject*. "Moreover, jurisdiction is essentially a relationship between a superior and determined subjects; but every relationship presupposes a second term and, consequently, if that term does not exist, jurisdiction also cannot exist" (Fr. X. Wernz, S.J., *Ius Decretalium*, II, 2 [Romae, 1906²], 529). If one is dealing with the power as regards some positive juridical disposition, then, according to the notion itself of power, a concrete subject must be determined. Such a determination, however, is not required when it is a question of power conferred sacramentally in episcopal consecration. In this case it is power in a theological sense, although of course ordained for the Church.

20. L. Hertling, S.J., in "Communio und Primat," *Miscellanea Historiae Pontificiae*, VII [Romae, 1943], 1–48, maintains that this idea was clearly already present in the Church of the earlier centuries. "The ancient Church was not made up of just a great number of like-minded bishops, a so to speak arithmetic sum; rather these bishops were held together by the solid bond of juridico-sacramental communion. It is this communion that really and truly constitutes the *una sancta ecclesia*. The center of the communion is the Church of Rome with its Bishop, and since this communion is a juridico-sacramental organism, its center is an effective sacral authority. Whomever the Bishop of Rome excludes from communion is no longer a member of the Church, and whomever he grants communion is by that fact a member of the Church. Each individual bishop can of course grant or refuse communion, but he can do this only when he acts as an agent of the entire Church; therefore, only when he is in communion with the entire Church and consequently in communion ultimately with its center, therefore, with Rome. The Bishop of Rome, however, does not need to base his power on communion with others: he is himself the source and origin of all communion" (*Ibid.*, 43 f.).

21. Cf. *supra*, n. 19.

22. If the Second Vatican Council should grant either bishops or conferences of bishops faculties to regulate the liturgy, such a concession would make it immediately clear that a major cause of its very nature is not in question.

23. The other opinion maintains that a dispensation from vows is a

major cause of its very nature. Hence the faculty of dispensing from vows that is conceded according to the norms of Canon 1313 is not a faculty of the episcopal office as constituted by divine law, but is conceded in its substance by the Holy See to the bishops. (We are prescinding from this particular question in the present context.) Nevertheless, even if we presuppose the first opinion, we cannot say in general that: "The full participation of a bishop in the duties and rights of the entire episcopacy is *de iure* to be presumed. . . . Thus, in this view it would be *iuris divini* that only as many of these rights belonging to the entire Episcopacy could be taken away from an individual bishop as could be shown to be right and just by the concrete circumstances" (Karl Rahner, S.J., *op. cit.*, p. 69). For if a particular cause could not be generally reserved to the Holy See (this text, however, does not maintain this), it would be impossible to have a major cause of positive law. Moreover, this fact would logically lead to the conclusion that the primatial power is not immediately an episcopal one over the entire Church.

24. Hence on the question whether the bishops' faculties for dispensing, granted by common law itself (e.g., the faculty of dispensing from matrimonial impediments in accordance with Canons 1043, 1045), constitute *ordinary power* or *delegations by the law*, B. Ojetti, S.J., rightly notes in his *Commentarium in Codicem Iuris Canonici* (De personis, Cans. 145–214 [Romae, 1931], pp. 164 ff.) that only that power should be considered ordinary power which is connected to an office by *constitutional* law. We can prescind from this question in the present context. We note, however, that Ojetti's opinion has at least this much of a foundation: we cannot deduce from a reference to a faculty of dispensation in the Code of Canon Law that the faculty is ordinary. It would be necessary to prove that such a faculty of dispensing belongs to the episcopal office as it is constituted by divine law. On the other hand, if such faculties do actually inhere in the episcopal office by constitutional (divine) law, the absolute possibility still remains that they are reserved to the Holy See. (Confer the preceding note.)

25. Actually canonical prescriptions on the part of episcopal conferences can be efficaciously accomplished throughout an entire region only if such prescriptions oblige all the bishops. In this regard juridical development during the Middle Ages is instructive. "About the middle of the ninth century the Metropolitans had actually assumed the position of intermediaries between the Pope and diocesan bishops as Boniface had planned. *The False Decretals* played a very essential part in this development since one of the purposes of Pseudo-Isidore was the strengthening of papal power. The concomitant danger, which Boniface had already recognized, of the Metropolitans attempting to exaggerate their independence in relation to Rome did, of course, become serious. But this movement met with impressive adversaries, not only the Pope but the diocesan bishops as well. . . . The actual development completely bypassed the Metropolitans. The Metropolitans would have had an effective countermeasure for the

assertion of their leading position in the provinces in provincial councils, but neither they, nor the bishops, as Hinschius has already shown, were inclined to tolerate the limitations connected with this institution for each party. And this factor contributed to the fact that such councils were less and less frequently convoked" (Plöchl, *op. cit.*, I, 307 f.).

26. Confer the Oriental legislation on physical and moral persons, Canons 216 and 240, in *Acta Apostolicae Sedis* 49 (1957), 497 and 504.

27. This position (on the historical title of patriarchal power) is defended by W. de Vries, S.J., in his "Die Entstehung der Patriarchate des Ostens und ihr Verhältnis zur päpstlichen Vollgewalt," *Scholastik* 37 (1962), 341–369.

28. Confer Fuchs, *op. cit.*, IV, 51 ff.

29. Confer Canon 6 of the First Council of Nicaea (*infra*, n. 31).

30. Confer the following note.

31. The First Ecumenical Council of Nicaea (325), Canon 4: "It is indeed most proper that a bishop be ordained by all the bishops in a province. But if this should prove difficult, either because of pressing need or because of the long trip, then the ordination would be performed by at least three of them when they have agreed on their candidate with the written approval of those who are absent. But let the confirmation of the proceedings be assigned to the Metropolitan bishops in each province." Canon 6: Let the ancient custom be preserved throughout Egypt, Libya, and the Pentapolis in accordance with which the Bishop of Alexandria has authority over all of them; for the Bishop of Rome has a similar practice. Similarly, however, let the Church in Antioch and the other provinces also preserve their privileges. But it is generally clear that, if an individual is made a bishop without the approval of the Metropolitan, the great synod declares that this man ought not to be a bishop. But if a common decision has been reached by all that is reasonable and confirmed according to ecclesiastical regulations, but two or three object because of personal contentiousness, the opinion of the majority would prevail" (Conradus Kirch, *Enchiridion Fontium Historiae Ecclesiasticae Antiquae*, [Friburgi Brisgoviae, 1923⁴] nn. 240 ff.).

32. Plöchl, *op. cit.*, I, 173 ff.

33. An illustration of this point, at least under a certain formal aspect, is afforded by the imposition of canonical form for the celebration of marriage only from the time of the very famous chapter "Tametsi" of the Council of Trent. We cannot conclude from this fact that the right of the Church to require canonical form for marriage did not exist before this time. Where there is no canonical prescription requiring canonical form, the mutual and properly given consent constitutes matrimony in its substance and existence, and the external structure naturally follows since the matrimonial rights are constituted to be exercised. But under the canonical prescription which demands canonical form, a marriage that lacks such form, even though the consent constitutes the matrimonial rights in their substance and existence, lacks that structure which is legally re-

quired in the Church. The marriage that lacks this structure lacks an essential element so that it is juridically inefficacious and, consequently, is simply invalid. Therefore it is justly said that: "Although, therefore, all ecclesiastical power flows from God, nevertheless it always presupposes Peter who has been appointed the foundation of the building, the bearer of the keys of the kingdom, and pastor of the universal flock" (C. Molari, "Adnotationes de natura potestatis hierarchicae Ecclesiae," *Divinitas* 6 [1962], 569).

34. In connection with this point there is certainly significance in the question of whether the distinction between priesthood of the first order (the episcopacy) and priesthood of the second order (the presbyterate) is of divine or human law. Moreover, to explain the priest's power of confirming and ordaining—which is had in certain cases by law or can be granted by the Roman Pontiff (perhaps even for sacramental orders)—the opinion is also proposed that in order to confer a sacrament the recipient must be a subject of the minister. In this sense jurisdiction is required for the administration of the sacraments. This jurisdiction is under the current legislation conferred upon all bishops for the valid administration of all sacraments. Priests, however, can acquire it from the Roman Pontiff for the sacraments of confirmation and orders. As a matter of fact the practice of the first centuries of the Church confirms this opinion inasmuch as the power of the Church used to be considered as a unity, but the execution of power was not considered valid unless ordination had been conferred for a determined church, i.e., unless the ordinee was coordinated with the exercise of the power of the rest of the clerics in the Church. In fact the Roman Pontiff can affect in this way the valid execution of even the power of orders by removing jurisdiction (which really occurs as the case in the sacrament of penance). On these questions confer H. Lennerz, S.J., *De sacramento ordinis* (Romae, 1947), pp. 83 ff., 144 ff.

35. Confer *supra*, Historical Prenotes.

36. Confer *supra*, Historical Prenotes.

37. Pius XII, *Constitutio Apostolica "Vacantis Apostolicae Sedis,"* Acta Apostolicae Sedis, 38 (1946), 97.

38. *Ibid.*, 98.

39. Confer *supra*, note 11.

40. "Consecration of the duly elected Pope as Bishop of Rome was necessary only as long as it was law and custom to elevate to the pontificate a non-bishop, thus a deacon or presbyter, or by way of exception, a layman. Anyone who was a bishop was to remain forever connected to his diocese as if in a kind of matrimonial bond, and was not to be transferred to another bishopric. The Roman Synod of 769 renewed this ancient prohibition: 'Oportebat, ut in apostolatus culmen unus de cardinalibus presbiteris aut diaconibus consecraretur.' Accordingly a directive in the *Ordo Romanus IX*, n. 5 (800–850): 'elegitur aut presbiter aut diaconus: nam episcopus esse non poterit. . . .' The election decree of 1059 § 3 repealed the possession of episcopal consecration as an impediment to election by permitting election *ex alia ecclesia*. In accordance with this the following

were appointed to the Papal dignity: Bishop Suidger of Bamberg as Clement II (1046); the Bishop of Toul as Leo IX (1049); the Bishop of Eichstatt as Victor II (1055); the Bishop of Siena as Nicholas II (1058). This addition occurs in Note 1 (from the *Annales Fuldenses* for the year 882): 'John, the Roman Pontiff, died; Marinus who was already a bishop took his place contrary to the statutes of the canons.' " (Eduard Eichmann, *Weihe und Krönung des Papstes im Mittelalter* [München, 1951], Münchener Theologische Studien, I, 3 ff.).

41. "The individual elected is called in the sources *electus* in contrast to the perfect, consecrated *episcopus* or *pontifex;* he is the chosen of God through the vote of the electors" (*Ibid.*, p. 5).

42. "In antiquity, until the pontiff-elect was consecrated, the power of conducting affairs used to remain in the hands of those who used to administer the Church when the See was vacant, or in the hands of the archpresbyter, archdeacon, and chancellor. There are very many historical documents extant on this point" (Felix M. Cappello, *De Curia Romana*, Vol. II: *De Curia Romana Sede Vacante* [Romae, 1912], 551).

43. This fact explains why Clement V (Cap. 4, extravag. comm., de sententia excommunicationis, V, 10 [ed. Friedberg, II] c. 1312) levied an excommunication against those who attack the acts performed by the Supreme Pontiff before his coronation. This excommunication is in force even under current legislation (Pius XII, *Constitutio Apostolica "Vacantis Apostolicae Sedis,"* A.A.S. 38 [1946], 97). Of itself the coronation of the Supreme Pontiff confers no spiritual power. Nevertheless a satisfactory explanation of the fact that non-coronation afforded the pretext for not accepting the administrative acts of a merely elected Supreme Pontiff is found in the ancient tradition that the Supreme Pontiff, if he did not have all the elements which constituted his creation, was not accustomed to exercise his power of governing. Consequently, such a penal norm makes clear the creation of the Supreme Pontiff as the head of the Church by God Himself from the very moment of his election and acceptance.

44. A subject is constituted "in the supreme pontificate by the divine law itself, on fulfillment of the condition of lawful election and acceptance of the same; in the other degrees of jurisdiction, by canonical mission" (Canon 109). Therefore in the elevation to the supreme pontificate of one who has already been consecrated a bishop—as generally happens today— the structure of the primatial power is quite clear, since his episcopal power which has already been substantially conferred becomes efficacious for the entire Church by his election and acceptance thereof.

An Unresolved Question on the Origin of the Episcopal Power of Jurisdiction in the Council of Trent

At the beginning of 1562 the third and final stage of the Council of Trent began. This stage lasted till the end of 1563 when the Council was dissolved with the final session on December 3 and 4. Among the questions keenly discussed during this stage was one which had already been deliberated upon in the first stage, the question of the residency of Bishops,[1] i.e., whether the obligation to residency arose from divine or ecclesiastical law. The promoters of the divine origin of this obligation were directly and especially aiming at the cessation of abuses that were caused by failure to observe residence. Nevertheless, this issue was considered linked with the question of the origin of episcopal power of jurisdiction, i.e., whether this power of jurisdiction is conferred immediately by God (through episcopal consecration) or through the Roman Pontiff. The latter aspect of this question complicated the main issue since it could be seen that it could easily give rise to some prejudice with regard to the primatial power.

The Fathers of the Council were almost evenly divided on this question.[2] Even the legates of the Roman Pontiff were divided in their views: Gonzaga and Seripando did not consider the question dangerous while Simonetta and Hosius strongly emphasized the aforementioned prejudice. It should be noted that foremost among the supporters of the divine right were the Spanish bishops, who otherwise forcefully rejected the accusation that they were attempting to diminish the authority of the Roman Pontiff.

The motion which Father James Lainez, then General of the Society of Jesus, made in the general congregation of October 20, 1562,[3] deserves special mention because it was considered one of the most significant of the Council and was both highly praised and attacked. He defended the view that the power of jurisdiction was conferred upon the bishops immediately by the Roman Pontiff. Then on December 9, 1562, Father Lainez proposed that there be no mention of the power of episcopal jurisdiction since both views were supported by many Catholics. Therefore, the only point that should be defined was that the bishops are, as far as orders are concerned, of divine law from Christ.[4] Of course, this proposition was not immediately accepted by everyone. But in the general congregation of July 9, 1563, decrees were passed concerning the sacrament of orders and residence. In the decree on the sacrament of orders discussion was limited to the episcopal order with no mention of the power of episcopal jurisdiction. Moreover, in the decree on residence no mention was made of the basis for this obligation.[5] Then in the 23rd session on July 15, 1563, these decrees were approved and promulgated in Chapter IV of the decree on the sacrament of orders[6] and in Canon 1 of the decree on the reformation[7] respectively. The Spanish bishops approved Chapter IV of the decree on the sacrament of orders because it was explicitly stated in this Chapter that the bishops were appointed by the

Holy Spirit to govern the Church of God, but these words could also be understood to agree with their opinion.[8]

1. FATHER LAINEZ' ARGUMENT

We do not intend to expound in these pages the Tridentine discussions on the question of the origin of the power of episcopal jurisdiction. Rather we are merely attempting to show that the principal arguments proposed by Fr. Lainez are based upon suppositions which cannot be considered genuine and, furthermore, that the principles that he advanced as necessary to be retained are completely preserved even if the other opinion is accepted.

The purpose of Father Lainez' motion was to protect the primatial power. He was afraid that this would not be safeguarded by the opinion that the power of jurisdiction is conferred in episcopal consecration. The following are the texts from his motions which bear out this point:

I was showing from the Fathers that they hold that the power of jurisdiction is completely lost. If, then, such is the case, it is not immediately from God, because, if it were, it could not be taken away and lost. It is clear from this, therefore, that it is from the Pope. . . .

This power is a certain relationship, and every relationship necessarily has its terms by the same right. Now, the terms are superior and subject. If, then, the bishops have this superiority by divine right, they have their subjects by divine right. But if the latter, then the subjects cannot be removed from them, or changed, or given by another; and this denies accepted facts, namely, that a diocese may be assigned by the Pope.

Likewise, if the bishops have this power by divine right, they have it either limitedly or unlimitedly. If limitedly, it can (not) be diminished or increased by the Pope; but if unlimitedly, it then includes every bit, and thus there is not just one prince in the Church of God, but as many princes as there are bishops.

Likewise, if they have this power by divine right, but do not have its exercise by the same right, there is an inconsistency since Christ gave this power which cannot be exercised in itself. (*C.T.* IX, 101)

And furthermore the bishops have jurisdiction before consecration when they are merely ordained and confirmed; therefore, it is not given in virtue of consecration, and it is decreed in Chapter II of the Council of Chalcedon that it must be shown before consecration that an individual has a title, that is, the care of souls. Therefore, the care of souls and, consequently, jurisdiction is given before consecration. Moreover, jurisdiction depends upon the will of the Pontiff; therefore, it is not given in the character. Likewise, if it were given in the character, each person would be given the same, neither greater nor less, and it could never be taken away, limited, or removed by the Pontiff since the Pontiff would not have power over a decree of Christ, nor can the power of the Pope take away the power of Christ. (*C.T.* IX, 225)

Let it be defined, therefore, that the bishops are, as far as orders are concerned, of divine law from Christ. But let no mention be made of jurisdiction since many Catholic Fathers defend both sides in this issue. For if it were to be proclaimed that the jurisdiction and superiority of the bishops over the presbyters is of divine law, the Pontiffs and the councils would not be able to release anyone from the jurisdiction of a bishop. For if it is given by Christ: neither men nor angels can increase, remove or lessen it. (*C.T.* IX, 225)

2. SOLUTION

We must agree completely with Fr. Lainez on the point that any opinion on the origin of the power of episcopal jurisdiction which would be damaging to the primatial power cannot be sound. Christ the Lord truly instituted the primatial power. Hence it would be impossible to have another power in the Church which as such would be damaging to this primatial power. And this must be all the more firmly asserted today than at the time of the Council of Trent since the First Vatican Council solemnly proclaimed that the Roman Pontiff enjoys episcopal power over the entire Church and is himself the Bishop of all bishops.[9] Therefore, among the criteria for the genuineness of a view on the origin of the power of episcopal jurisdiction, the last place is not to be assigned to the harmoniousness of such a view with the primatial power.

Nonetheless, Fr. Lainez' assertion that the conferral of the power of jurisdiction in episcopal consecration is damaging to the primatial power can and should be denied. The Spanish bishops, themselves, while maintaining the view that the power of jurisdiction is conferred in episcopal consecration, were no doubt sincere when they said that they did not wish to derogate from the primatial power in any way. For the devotion which the Church of Spain has always fostered for the Holy See is renowned. Besides, they could rightly appeal, on the one hand, to an ancient tradition in this affair,[10] and, on the other, to the fact that the opinion, that the exclusive conferral of the power of episcopal jurisdiction was effected by an act separate from episcopal consecration, had not been proposed until the High Middle Ages.

For this opinion supposes the reflex distinction between the power of orders and the power of jurisdiction, a distinction which was not had until the middle of the twelfth century.[11] Previously, the episcopal power was viewed as a unity of those faculties[12] which were required for the administration of the episcopal office, namely, for the formal performance of worship, for the administration of the sacraments, for the preaching of the word of God, for the direction of the Christian people, etc. Nevertheless, to preserve order in the exercise of sacred power in the Church the administration of the episcopal office demanded, in addition to episcopal consecration itself,[13] what was termed an "execution."[14] This is the explanation of the fact that in all orders the execution of the power received in ordination was not possessed if the ordination itself was absolutely conferred. In this sense, at least, absolute ordination was null.[15] Execution, therefore, presupposes ordination for a determined Church. When an ecclesiastical office is had, right order is preserved in the exercise of sacred power.

Nevertheless, despite the prohibition of absolute ordination, this practice compelled recognition at the end of the Middle Ages. Indeed, it was ultimately accepted as legal. Consequently, the danger was present that the power conferred in ordination might be exercised outside of right order, i.e., without this exercise being subject to any ecclesiastical authority. Therefore, the function of preserving right order in the Church, which assignment to a determined church in ordination itself once performed, now had to be performed in another way. Consequently, execution was henceforth conferred by a special commission on the part of ecclesiastical authority. There was question, however, of whether or not such a commission was required for the exercise of each and every power received in ordination. This question arose because ordination which was illegal in a special way, namely, ordination conferred by a heretic, was not considered completely null, although there was not yet complete clarity on this issue—such as there was from the time of St. Augustine with regard to the baptism of heretics. For it is well known that up to the time of the Gregorian Reform (in the eleventh and twelfth centuries) renowned authors were of the opinion that simoniacal ordination, since it was heretical, was completely null and conferred no power.[16]

Such difficulties were only gradually solved by means of the practice of the Church so that finally Stephanus Tornacensis, the decretist, could propose a solution about the year 1160: The absolutely ordained can celebrate Mass privately and confect the sacraments themselves, but he cannot publicly perform the sacred ministries for the Christian people. By the sacred ministries are understood all the ministries which are exercised in caring for souls. Accordingly, then, there is present for the first time in some real way a distinction between the power of orders and the power of jurisdiction,[17] since the power of orders can of itself always be validly exercised, but everything which makes up the public ministry in behalf of the community of faithful, requires a special commission from a competent ecclesiastical superior.

As far as the word jurisdiction is concerned, it did not yet have a specific meaning either in Gratian or in the earlier decretists. Rather this technical term was used in a specific sense during the first part of the thirteenth century. From this time on the distinction between the power of orders and the power of jurisdiction was common in the sense that has become traditional for centuries.[18] The power of orders is acquired by ordination so that it can always be validly exercised and never lost. The power of jurisdiction is validly possessed only by commission on the part of ecclesiastical authority and can be taken away or restricted by the same authority. It should be noted, however, that the lawful (that is licit) exercise of the power of orders is always subject to the power of jurisdiction of the respective ecclesiastical superior.

Nevertheless, once this distinction was admitted in theory and practice in the Church, its origin and development was almost immediately consigned to oblivion. Moreover the very structure of the episcopal power no longer received any attention as long as its unity was not sufficiently manifested. It is of course true that as regards the episcopacy[19] the ancient tradition of consecrating a candidate for a determined Church (a diocese) continued, as it does to the present day so that non-residential bishops themselves are consecrated to the title of a diocese which was once existent and is now extinct. Nonetheless, even as regards the episcopacy the power of jurisdiction was no longer held to be conferred with episcopal consecration itself, but by a special commission, which under existing legislation is termed a canonical mission (Can. 109) or canonical institution (Can. 332, § 1). Accordingly, conferral of ordination and conferral of an office in the Church, which were effected by one and the same act in the time of relative ordination, were effected, after absolute ordination was accepted, by separate juridical acts, namely, ordination and conferral of office.

Roman law which had a renaissance in the Middle Ages exercised a great influence on the development of the theory of office in the Church. A civil office of Roman law consists in public power or the power of placing juridical acts in the name of the entire community or of the Roman people. With the conferral of office this power is conferred in its substance and exercise. Actually the power of the Church is not derived from the community of the faithful, but from the Lord Himself. Supposing this difference, the understanding of Roman law was accepted by the canonists, since the power of jurisdiction is exercised in the name of the Church. Consequently the power of jurisdiction is considered conferred by the conferral of office, not only in its exercise but also in its substance. Such an understanding was all the more easily sanctioned because some power is also derived from ordination, namely the power of orders.[20] (Moreover, the power of jurisdiction can also be conferred without conferring an office, but in the Church the office properly speaking is primarily constituted by the very power of jurisdiction.)

In this sense, therefore, the very ancient tradition, extending from the High Middle Ages back to the time of the Apostles, looked upon all episcopal power as a unit conferred in episcopal consecration itself; this met with no little obscurity. Doubtless, according to the exposition given above, episcopal consecration as such was not sufficient previously for the exercise of the power received. Rather to have "execution" of episcopal power, i.e., for the efficacious possession of an office in the Church, the assignment of a particular, determined Church was necessary. Nevertheless, the power itself was not held to have been conferred with this assignment, but rather the juridical efficacy of the power or office respectively which was received in episcopal consecration. On the contrary, from the high Middle Ages onward, canonical mission or canonical institution in the case of bishops was conceived of as the conferral of the very power of jurisdiction, even of the very episcopal office, at least insofar as this was a canonical office.[21]

Granted these facts, the analysis of the opinion proposed by Fr. Lainez is obvious. He simply assumed not merely a distinction but also a division between the power of orders and the power of jurisdiction. The power of jurisdiction is had in bishops through an injunction, i.e., through the conferral of this very power on the part of the Roman Pontiff. For if the power of jurisdiction should be immediately conferred by God, according to Fr. Lainez, the Roman Pontiff could neither restrict nor remove it.[22] Furthermore, the necessity, which at one time demanded the application of the candidate to a determined particular Church or diocese for reception of episcopal consecration, was viewed by Fr. Lainez as the necessity of having a diocese already, thus jurisdiction before episcopal consecration.

3. THE PREFERABLE HISTORICO-CANONICAL EXPLANATION

Moreover, this assertion in particular makes it clear that such an understanding does not agree with the historical facts because in former times of relative ordination, it was simply impossible to conceive of the possession of any power prior to episcopal consecration. But as far as the necessity of a dependence of the power of episcopal jurisdiction on primatial power is concerned, this must doubtlessly be affirmed and defended from all infringement. Analysis of the historical facts affords all the elements to do this, although these facts actually show that the conferral of episcopal power was effected in episcopal consecration. For the conferral of episcopal consecration for a determined, particular church includes the formality of incorporation of the consecrated bishop within the hierarchical Church, within the hierarchy itself of the Church, i.e., it includes the formality of coordination of the power received in consecration with other bishops who legitimately enjoy the power of governing in the Church.

This is why a bishop consecrated absolutely is not incorporated within the Church. His consecration is null so that he cannot enjoy any execution of his episcopal

108

power. Consequently it is really impossible to conceive of episcopal power as independent from the primatial power, not even during the entire period when the Roman Pontiff did not grant, either by himself or through his delegate (a Metropolitan), the episcopal office in individual cases by a special act. The Roman Pontiff played a part in the creation of bishops since the law or custom to be observed could not be lawful unless it were accepted by him. Moreover, it is the Roman Pontiff's function to control the juridical and efficacious exercise of the power of jurisdiction that has been received. Hence for proportionately grave reasons affecting the common good of the Church, he can restrict or take away episcopal power, i.e., impede the juridical efficacy and thereby the validity of the exercise of power.

Fr. Lainez' argument, i.e., power conferred in consecration which could not be exercised is utterly useless, calls for the following comments. Such a statement reveals that Fr. Lainez was paying no attention to the finality of the episcopal power conferred in consecration. For this power is ordered to the Church, is conferred for the Church, and is to be exercised in the Church. This power cannot be considered as if it were constituted for itself alone and to be exercised independently of every tie. Accordingly, the power received, but still not incorporated within the Church, really suffers from a lack of subjects and, consequently, it cannot be exercised.[23]

It can justly be said, therefore, that at the time of the Council of Trent it was impossible to reduce both opinions on the origin of the power of episcopal jurisdiction to a commonly accepted opinion. The supporters of the view that power of jurisdiction was conferred in episcopal consecration could appeal to an ancient tradition on this point.

Yet, since they paid no attention to the "execution" which was required in antiquity for the (valid) exercise of episcopal power, they were not able to give an adequate explanation of the dependence of the power of episcopal jurisdiction upon the primatial power—and they in no way denied this dependence. Father Lainez, however, in his defence of the contrary opinion did not meet the demands of the Church's most ancient tradition. With such a state of the question, it is easily understood that the issue itself could not be solved. For both views contained some truth; but the difficulty lay in reconciling the true elements that were latent in both opinions.

The solution to the difficulty, therefore, in terms of ancient and current positive law is had in the fact that the assignment of a particular church (diocese) in episcopal consecration itself includes the formality of incorporation of the consecrated bishop within the hierarchy of the Church. Under current legislation the canonical mission or institution corresponds to this assignment of a particular church. In either case such incorporation renders juridically efficacious the power of jurisdiction conferred in consecration that is consequently dependent upon the Roman Pontiff for its valid exercise.[24]

4. SPECULATIVE EXPLANATION

A further speculative explanation of this solution is had in the fact that what is theologically and canonically established about the conferral of episcopal power is explained by a reduction to the metaphysical principles concerning sociability and law in the concrete, supernatural order.

Social life, as befits the spiritual-corporeal nature of

man, is made up of two elements, an internal and an external one. Hence social and juridical activity is formally intentional activity which is manifested and becomes externally efficacious (by means of corporeal activity). Since the respective intentional relations are ordered to the actuation of human values themselves, they constitute the internal structure of both sociability and law; this internal structure becomes externally efficacious by means of an external structure. It should be noted that the external structure, although it does not constitute the substance of the juridical activity, does constitute an essential element of it because men are not capable of merely internal communication.

Furthermore, it should be noted that personal activity as such cannot be affected by organized society, such as the State and the Church, because the person itself, its destiny as such, together with its rights and duties that are founded on personality, are antecedent to and independent of organized society. It is instead the function of such a society to regulate (organize) within its own competence and for the sake of the common good juridical activity insofar as this effects the social life itself. Hence juridical activity which is not in accord with the common good can be denied recognition. Consequently, the recognized effects of such activity in society are not had. The efficacy of juridical activity which is not recognized by organized society exists only to the degree in which the society itself cannot impede it. The causality of personal juridical activity brings about the constitution of a right itself in its substance or its intentional being and internal structure. But this right thus constituted is not incorporated within society. In order that society may be able to order efficaciously the exercise of rights which properly constitutes the end

of organized society, it should and does have influence over
the external structure of a right thus constituted, inasmuch
as it places an obstacle to its external structure so that the
causality of juridical activity, which of itself extends
through the internal structure to the external structure of
the right to be constituted, cannot bring about the external
structure. The substantially constituted right, because of a
defect of recognition and incorporation within society,
lacks the requisite external structure. Therefore it lacks
an essential element and is, consequently, not completely
constituted.

Accordingly, by this secure arrangement the independence of personal juridical activity as such from organized
society is preserved, since this activity makes up the sole
and adequate causality of the constitution of rights. This
society's competence over the exercise of the fundamental
rights of men is preserved by the fact that the faculty of
incorporating or not incorporating the rights to be constituted within social life is truly appropriated to it. If
this incorporation is lacking, the right is not constituted
completely since it lacks an essential element, namely,
the requisite external structure. The unity of the right to
be constituted is safeguarded because only that right which
is completely constituted is efficacious and can be exercised.
Moreover, the external structure of the right is the transposition of the internal structure to the outside. It is not
an external accretion to a constituted right.

On these suppositions it is easy to explain how the
power of jurisdiction can be so conferred in episcopal consecration that it is juridically inefficacious as long as it is
not recognized by the Roman Pontiff. Since episcopal consecration does not produce union with the rest of the
bishops, i.e., incorporate the power conferred within the

hierarchy of the Church, it is not sufficient of itself to empower the consecrated bishop to exercise episcopal power in the Church validly. Consequently, if the Pope has not recognized the conferral of episcopal power, this power lacks its requisite external structure, although it is certainly substantially conferred. Hence it is not efficaciously possessed and cannot be exercised.

Although the Church cannot touch the causality as such of episcopal consecration itself—since it is the vicarious action of Christ—it most certainly can touch this causality inasmuch as it bears upon the external, social, juridical life of the Church, i.e., inasmuch as the power, constituted through consecration, is made efficacious. Because the efficacy of episcopal power, substantially conferred in consecration, is not recognized, an external obstacle is placed to the transposition of the internal structure of such a power to the outside. Without the requisite external structure the power itself is not completely constituted; it is not efficacious and cannot be exercised. Such a structure manifests the relation of episcopal power to the Church. For Christ the Lord instituted the episcopal office and constantly produces it anew in the candidates for the episcopacy that it be exercised in the Church and not apart from communion with the Church.[25]

In the light of these statements, an explanation is afforded of the entire historical development of episcopal creation. Invariably episcopal power has been, is, and will be given in episcopal consecration. This power is a whole containing the power of orders and the power of jurisdiction. This power is ordered to the Church. As long as it is not incorporated within the Church, its exercise is unlawful, and indeed, as far as the power of jurisdiction is concerned, invalid or juridically inefficacious because the exercise of the power of jurisdiction of its very nature directly affects social life.[26] In early traditions such incorporation was had through lawful (i.e., approved by the Metropolitan and the co-provincial bishops) episcopal consecration for a determined particular church (diocese); then in the Middle Ages (by the Law of the Decretals) by the Metropolitan's confirmation of a candidate who was canonically elected by the cathedral chapter; finally, by canonical mission and institution on the part of the Roman Pontiff.

Thus the explanation of the entire historical development of episcopal creation is actually derived from the same principle. But if it is supposed that the power of jurisdiction, itself, comes from the Roman Pontiff and, consequently, is in no way conferred in episcopal consecration, it is impossible to explain the Church's practice up to the High Middle Ages. The Church for an entire millennium considered episcopal power to be conferred by episcopal consecration; furthermore, during this time the conferral of the power of jurisdiction by some special act was not even thought of and, consequently, cannot be explained through a tacit concession. On the other hand, it is clear from these statements that no norm for the creation of a bishop which was not accepted by the Roman Pontiff was ever lawful, and there was never an exemption from the primatial power in regard to the valid exercise of power of jurisdiction of any bishop. Accordingly, under this concept what must be preserved is truly preserved and what must be explained is truly explained. Thus our assertions are also confirmed by the entire historico-canonical development up to the present in the *Code of Canon Law* itself: the episcopal office "of ruling the Church of God" (Acts 20:28) was instituted by Christ the Lord, and must be sacramentally conferred that it may be exercised in communion with the Roman Pontiff in the Church entrusted to him "to the building up of the body of Christ—which is the Church—in love" (Eph. 4:16; Col. 1:24).

Notes

1. Confer the history of the last stage of the Council of Trent in Ludwig von Pastor, *The History of the Popes*, XV (ed. R. F. Kerr), 264–378. Hubert Jedin in his *Krisis und Wendepunkt des Trienter Konzils* (Würzburg, 1941) throws new light on the resolution of the question of episcopal residency. "As a matter of fact the problem had arisen at the beginning of the Council and was concerned precisely with pastoral needs. Actually since the end of 1546, when there was question of introducing into the law diverse measures—in practice financial sanctions—to oblige bishops and others who had the care of souls to reside among their flocks (measures which ran a very high risk, as events would show, of having no more efficacy than the other previous directives), several Spanish bishops had requested that this obligation to residence be declared to be of divine law and, consequently, outside the Roman dispensations which were destructive of all attempts at reform. Some publications of Spanish theologians, B. Carranza, D. Soto, B. Torrès, had just offered timely support of these theses which had already been defended in 1517 by Cardinal Cajetan in his commentary on the *Secunda Secundae*" (A. Duval, "L'ordre au concile de Trente," in *Études sur le sacrement de l'ordre*, [Paris, 1957], p. 306).

2. In the general congregation of April 20, 1562, a ballot was taken on the question of whether the Fathers "wish or do not wish residency to be declared to be of divine law." The balloting took the following form: Not acceptable unless His Holiness is consulted. Acceptable. Not acceptable. Acceptable, after His Holiness' mind is known. "For the affirmative there were 66 votes. For the simple negative or for the negative with some addition or with referral to his Holiness there were 71 votes." There were also a few other votes which are not accounted for here. *Concilium Tridentinum*, Editio Goerresiana, VIII [Friburgi Br., 1919] 463–465. (Hereafter referred to as *C.T.*)

3. *C.T.*, IX (1924), 94–101 (on the seventh canon on the sacrament of orders).

4. *C.T.*, IX, 225.

5. *C.T.*, IX, 601 f. "The conference of July 6 is the turning point of the Council. In it the dispute which had split and disabled the assembly for ten months was happily settled. More precisely a decision which was

not yet dogmatically ripe for definition by the Council was left to further theological discussion. This remedy, which was from the historical viewpoint of the history of dogma undoubtedly most fortunate, was able to be taken with the help of Lorraine. Its part in the negotiations towards agreement was, as the legates frankly admitted, decisive. The deadlock was finally broken. The session scheduled for July 15 could take place" (Jedin, op. cit., p. 90).

6. C.T., IX, 621, Denzinger-Schönmetzer, Enchiridion symb. nn. 1768 and 1777.

7. C.T., IX, 623–625; Conciliorum Oecumenicorum Decreta, ed. Centro di Documentazione Instituto per le Scienze Religiose (Bologna, 1962), pp. 720–722.

8. It is clear from the work of Carolus Antonius de Manentibus (Tractatus de potestate episcopali [Romae, 1726], dedicated to Benedict XIII) that this interpretation has some foundation. In this work the author declares that the power of governing is conferred upon bishops by consecration. He adduces many arguments from the Council of Trent to prove his thesis (pp. 97–182).

9. Denzinger-Schönmetzer, n. 3060.

10. This, for example, is stated by the Archbishop of Granada (among the written votes given between October 13 to 20, 1562): "It is a most certain truth which was never called into question by the Fathers of old that the bishops are the successors of the Apostles. The councils and Fathers have expressed themselves unconditionally and without distinguishing on this subject. Who has, then, granted the power to distinguish that they are successors in this, namely, orders, but not in that, namely, jurisdiction? What kind of succession would this be? And if the episcopacy is not an order, or if it is not of divine law that the episcopacy is an order, and if the holy synod does not define this, and if the bishops are superior to the presbyters only by the episcopacy, then they do not surpass them in orders, are not superior, and even in jurisdiction (as they say) they are not superior by divine law. . . . And it is also evident from this assertion and definition that nothing at all is being taken from the Supreme Pontiff, and there is not the slightest derogation from his dignity and superiority when we actually concede him everything that the others do who deny that the bishops have been completely and utterly instituted by divine law" (C.T., IX, 49). "And furthermore, when any bishop is elected Supreme Pontiff, either by Cardinals, or by the clergy or by the people according to the times, from whom does he obtain the supreme power of jurisdiction? From Christ, of course. Therefore, the bishops—no matter by whom they may also be elected, be it the Supreme Pontiff, or the clergy, or the people— have from the same Christ, by means of that election, the power of jurisdiction. For the one is just as spiritual as the other, and granted that one is more esteemed and greater, it is not, however, of another genus since there is one giver and author of both of them, the Lord" (C.T., IX, 50).

"It is enough that the Supreme Pontiff is the distributor of the entire matter [jurisdiction] so that no one can have it without him and thus cannot exercise an act of jurisdiction. . . . He is, moreover, the universal minister and superior to everyone" (C.T., IX, 50).

11. And then only in fact; the terms were not yet used. Confer n. 17.

12. Confer Matthäus Kaiser, *Die Einheit der Kirchengewalt nach dem Zeugnis des Neuen Testamentes und der Apostolischen Väter* (München, 1956), especially pp. 137 f. and 143. Cf. Richard A. Strigl, *Grundfragen der kirchlichen Ämterorganisation* (München, 1960), pp. 8 ff.

13. The development of the view that episcopal consecration was not part of the sacrament of orders was possible only after recognition of the reflex distinction between the power of orders and the power of jurisdiction. There can be no doubt that the Church from the very beginning maintained that episcopal consecration was sacramental. (Cf. Kaiser, *op. cit.*, pp. 121 ff.) It should be noted that the medieval canonists always held that episcopal consecration was part of the sacrament of orders. But we prescind in the present context from all the other questions which arise under this heading, e.g., the question of whether the distinction between the priesthood of the first order (the episcopacy) and the priesthood of the second order (the presbytcrate) is of divine or of ecclesiastical law.

14. "We have not yet clearly said what this 'executio' was. Normally it was received at the time of ordination: 'officium et executionem sui officii ex consecratione adipiscitur.' . . . In conclusion, it seems to us like a notion of the jurisdictional order: permission, qualification to exercise the order received (G. Fransen, "La tradition des canonistes du moyen âge," in *Études sur le sacrement de l'ordre* [Paris, 1957], pp. 267 f.).

15. Canon 6 of the Council of Chalcedon (451) in *Gratiani Decretum*, p. I, dist. 70, c. 1 (ed. Ae. Friedberg, I), 257: "The full exercise of the priesthood requires therefore the 'executio' which is on a par with 'populum sibi subjectum' or again 'conventum habere,' that is to say, 'populum convenientem ad sacramenta recipienda.' Degraded priests and bishops retain only the 'character' and lose 'executio': 'potestatem acceptam sacramento tenus retinent, effectus suae potestatis prorsus privantur.' This explains why priests who were ordained by simonists did not receive the 'executio.' The person who ordained them could only give what he had; all that was left to him was the 'sacramentum ordinis,' but he had lost the 'executio ordinis' and the 'virtus sacramenti.' These priests were, therefore, really priests, but they could not exercise the orders received. Was this an interdict, or was the exercise of orders invalid? We believe that only the first solution corresponds to the texts" (Fransen, *op. cit.*, pp. 266 f.).

16. Confer the previous note. For discussions among the authors of the validity of absolute and simoniacal ordination, confer Vinzenz Fuchs, *Der Ordinationstitel von seiner Entstehung bis auf Innozenz III* (Bonn, 1930), pp. 238–267; Agostino Fliche, *La Riforma Gregoriana e La Riconquista Cristiana* (Torino, 1959), pp. 339–353.

17. Klaus Morsdorf, "Die Entwicklung der Zweigliedrigkeit der kirchlichen Hierarchie," in *Münchener Theologische Zeitschrift* (1951), pp. 10 ff.; Strigl, *op. cit.*, pp. 13 ff.

18. "Analysis . . . shows three stages of development in the formation of the notion of jurisdiction from 1140 to 1250. In the first period, from Gratian (1140) to Siccardus de Cremona inclusive (1180), the canonists make almost no use of the word *jurisdiction*, and diocesan law, a synonymous expression, assigned jurisdiction the meaning of temporal and spiritual administrative power in general. The power of orders is not clearly distinguished from the power of jurisdiction, nor are these powers defined. In the second period, from Huguccio (1188) to Joannes Teutonicus inclusive (1210), the use of the word *jurisdiction* is more frequent. . . . Therefore, jurisdiction assumes the prevalent meaning of just spiritual administrative power and takes in acts that depend upon the power of orders. In the third period, from the Fourth Lateran Council (1215) to Bernard de Bottone inclusive (1250), the word *jurisdiction* is common among the canonists. They did not ascribe to the law of jurisdiction the technical value of synonymous jurisdiction, but after 1215 they clearly distinguish with Master Ambrose the power of orders from the power of jurisdiction, and with the exclusion of the administration of temporalities, ascribe to it the meaning of the public power of governing a perfect community" (M. Van de Kerckhove, "De notione iurisdictionis apud Decretistas et priores Decretalistas," in *Ius Pontificium* [1938], pp. 12 f.).

19. Just as formerly the prohibition of absolute ordination was also, or rather especially, in force for episcopal ordination, so also at the present time the principle that the power of jurisdiction is acquired by a special act, which is distinct from ordination, is also applied to the power of episcopal jurisdiction.

20. Strigl, *op. cit.*, pp. 14 ff.

21. There is no need to mention that such a concept has since then influenced canonical legislation, namely the Law of the Decretals. There is no doubt that the codification of law for canonical practice is very valuable. Nevertheless, there is also the ever present danger of no longer paying careful attention to the very development and structure of institutions. The remarks which Ulrich Stutz makes in his *Der Geist des Codex iuris canonici* (Stuttgart, 1918) on the codification of canon law by the Code of Canon Law, are generally applicable: "The first and indubitable result of every codification is a copious outpouring of the most genuinely dull and meaningless jurisprudence. Everyone plunges into the lawbook and believes that it is all he needs. Literal interpretation and knowledge of paragraphs are the only concerns in the beginning. The supposition is that the older law and jurisprudence are dispensable and can be thrown overboard as superfluous ballast" (p. 168).

22. At present invalid juridical acts are commonly distinguished into nonexistent acts (if an element necessary for the constitution of the substance of the act is lacking) and inefficacious acts (if the fulfilment of a

condition or formality, i.e., an element extrinsic to the substantially constituted act, is lacking). This distinction is had in the *Code of Canon Law;* confer Canon 1680, § 1, and Canon 1139, § 1. Actually an organized society can have no influence over the constitutive elements of an act when juridical acts which have been established by natural law or divine positive law are in question. It can, however, have influence over the efficacy of an act through the imposition of a condition or formality. Lacking this distinction, Father Lainez thought that, once the power of jurisdiction was constituted, its valid exercise could not be affected by the Church and, hence, could not be restricted or taken away. The same reason is behind his denial of the Church's power to introduce canonical form for the constitution of a valid marriage. Since the efficient cause of marriage is exclusively the consent of the parties, he thought that, once this consent was present, a valid marriage was present, because he was completely unaware of the possibility of the Church's influence upon the efficacy—and thus upon the validity—of the marriage. Cf. Herbert Oberhofer, *Die Ansicht des P. Lainez über die geheimen Ehen auf dem Konzil von Trient* (Meran, 1952), pp. 104–108. On the structure of the juridical act, cf. Olisius Robleda, "Nullitas actus iuridici in *Codice Iuris Canonici," Perodica de re morali, canonica, liturgica,* 35 (1946), 29 ff. *Idem,* "De conceptu actus iuridici," *ibid.* 51 (1962), 413 ff., 437 ff.

23. Therefore it is justly said, "These two examples, which are chosen rather because of their brevity than because of the notoriety of the personages in question and their influence in the discussions, suffice to show by their very divergence what the major problem of the council was: that of a theology of the Church, that of a theology of the 'apostolic' function, in the strong sense of the word, in the Church, and of its transmission and its differentiations. They also show why this investigation could not succeed at that very moment. For the theologians and bishops remained deeply divided on some particularly important points" (Duval, *op. cit.,* p. 305).

24. Consequently, the conferral of jurisdiction upon bishops that is spoken of in current legislation can be used in the following true sense. If the bishop has not received canonical institution from the Roman Pontiff, he does not enjoy the exercise of his power of jurisdiction. Furthermore, faculties can also be granted to him that do not form part of the episcopal office as it was constituted by divine law. Moreover, the distinction between ordinary and delegated power retains a true meaning inasmuch as it at least refers to the (valid) exercise of the power of jurisdiction. These questions need no further explanation in the present context. We merely wished to note that the prescriptions of current legislation on this matter constitute no difficulty for the solution here proposed to this question.

25. Confer the further development of this point in the first two sections of this work.

26. On the contrary, the exercise of the power of orders as such does not directly touch the social life. Perhaps this is the explanation why—

according to present common opinion—the power of orders, when validly conferred, can always be validly exercised. Of course the power of orders can be impeded by a defect of the power of jurisdiction, as in the sacrament of penance. Furthermore, there are authors who believe that the power of jurisdiction is necessary in the administration of the other sacraments also, when the case involves the exercise of power upon a person who ought to be a subject of the minister. We can prescind from these questions in the present context. But we can note that, supposing this position, we have a new reason why the power of jurisdiction conferred in episcopal consecration is never useless, because it would be efficacious in every case in which the Church has always considered the exercise of the power of orders to be lawful, e.g., in the case of sacramental absolution in danger of death.

The Collegiality of the Episcopacy

INTRODUCTION: METHOD

The question of the collegiality of the episcopal body was one of the much discussed topics at the second session of the Second Vatican Council. Scarcely anyone denied that the body of bishops constitutes a college. The further explanation of this collegiality does, however, involve controversy.

Perhaps an explanation of the power of governing—namely, the power of jurisdiction made up of *magisterium* and *imperium*—which the bishops enjoy, can make some contribution toward the solution of this problem. Since the bishops have this power to exercise not only personally but also corporately, at least in an Ecumenical Council, the Church has always held and proposed principles on this subject. Accordingly, the conclusions which follow from these principles, without explicitly treating the question under the formal aspect of collegiality, furnish an explanation of the collegiate nature of the episcopal body almost as corollaries to such principles.[1]

The mystery of the Church also includes the episcopacy as a supernatural reality. Consequently, although the episcopal power of governing in the Church is defined in juridical notions and principles, nonetheless it must be made completely clear that juridical notions and principles cannot adequately express the supernatural reality itself which is the episcopacy. Moreover, in order that juridical notions and principles may be genuinely applied in the Church, they always need to be reduced to the theological foundation in question. For although the Church is a human, public, and consequently truly juridical society, its supernatural character must always be taken into consideration. The juridical disposition of the Church is specified by a supernatural end. Hence the questions about the episcopacy must finally be solved from the theological nature of the subject. In order to make a genuine representation of this nature attention must be paid to all of the elements contained in Sacred Scripture, Tradition, and in the Church's practice, liturgy, and legislation from the very beginning. Analysis of the notions and prescriptions of positive law and their application to the episcopacy cannot by themselves lead to well-founded conclusions.

We would like to note, however, that we do not intend to propose in these pages the theological, historical, and canonical argumentation for the bishops' power of governing. Rather we intend to demonstrate that the two fundamental contrary positions on this issue can be reduced to a common principle. This principle truly constitutes a genuine synthesis of these positions because it adopts the essentials of both positions and reduces them to one. The proof of the genuineness of this principle lies in its agreement with the tradition of the Church, dating from the very beginning, and in its satisfying the theological and canonical exigencies that must be considered in this question.

Episcopal Jurisdiction at the Council of Trent

It is well known that the question of the origin of the bishops' jurisdiction was the subject of vehement debate at the Council of Trent. The question was whether the bishops' power of jurisdiction was conferred immediately by God (through episcopal consecration) or mediately, namely, through the Roman Pontiff. Both views found favor with about half of the Fathers of the Council and the legates of the Roman Pontiff were themselves in disagreement on this issue. It should be noted that the supporters of the divine right of episcopal power were principally the Spanish bishops who nonetheless strongly rejected the accusation that they were aiming at derogating in the least from the Roman Pontiff's authority. The other position was principally defended in the very famous report of Father James Lainez, at that time General of the Society of Jesus, in the General Congregation of October 20, 1562. His purpose was to protect the primatial power. For he was afraid that this would not be safeguarded in the position that maintained that the power of jurisdiction was conferred in episcopal consecration.

It is not our purpose in the present context to treat of the Tridentine discussions on this question, ultimately never settled. Furthermore, it can be said that such a question was incapable of settlement at that time. For it is true that any opinion on the origin of the power of episcopal jurisdiction that would be damaging to the primatial power cannot be sound. For Christ the Lord instituted the primatial power. Hence it would be impossible to have another power in the Church which as such would be damaging to this primatial power. And this must be all the more firmly asserted today than at the time of the Council of Trent because the first Vatican Council solemnly proclaimed that the Roman Pontiff enjoys episcopal power over the entire Church and is himself the bishop of all bishops. Therefore, among the criteria for the genuineness of a view on the origin of the power of episcopal jurisdiction, the last place is not to be assigned to the harmoniousness of such a view with the primatial power. On the other hand the Spanish bishops could justly appeal to ancient tradition in support of their opinion.

Hence we must admit that neither position on the origin of the bishops' power of jurisdiction, as presented at the Council of Trent, constitutes a principle which reductively includes the complete development of the creation of a bishop from the beginning to current legislation. The opinion defending the exclusive conferral of the power of jurisdiction through episcopal consecration does not explain the necessity of communion of the consecrated bishop with the hierarchy of the Church or, in particular, the dependence of this power upon the primatial power for its exercise, although such dependence was explicitly recognized at the Council of Trent. The opinion defending an injunction of such power exclusively through the Roman Pontiff does not explain the understanding and practice of the Church until the high Middle Ages. For during all this time such an injunction by means of a positive act, separate from episcopal consecration, was not even considered. Hence it cannot be said that such a concession (as distinctly conceived) was implicitly had through the primatial power.

It is true, however, that during this entire time "execution" was necessary for the lawful exercise of any order received. The ordinary way of obtaining this "execution"

124

was by ordination for a determined, particular church, so that with the possession of a church the exercise of the order received was lawful. The "execution," therefore, contained for the lawfully consecrated bishop the formality of incorporation within the hierarchy of the Church or the formality—as we say today (cf. Can. 109)—"of the canonical mission," by which are constituted the communion of the consecrated bishop with the hierarchy of the Church and his dependence upon the primatial power.

The change in the Church's practice in this regard is due to the change of law regarding absolute ordination, i.e., ordination that is not conferred for a particular, determined church. Absolute ordination was forbidden until the twelfth century. Then it was accepted so that thereafter the conferral of orders and the conferral of office, previously effected by one and the same act, took place in separate and distinct acts. Finally, only from this time do we find the reflex distinction between the power of orders and the power of jurisdiction that was commonly accepted in the thirteenth century. Previously, however, the episcopal power was considered as a single and authoritative whole with several functions corresponding to various offices of the Church (the power of orders and the power of jurisdiction taken together, not distinguished as such).

This historical development was almost unknown at the time of the Council of Trent. Hence it was not possible to reconcile the two views expressed at the Council into a unit. Furthermore, we must admit that only more recent historical studies have shed more light on this historical development[2] so that there is certainly no doubt at present but that the Church, during the entire first millennium, nullified the exercise of the power of governing that was

125

received through unlawful, because absolute, ordination. For the "execution" was not conferred upon the person who was unlawfully ordained. His ordination was not recognized since, as an ordinee, he was not incorporated within the Church. Thus he did not have the exercise of the power received in ordination.

Synthesis of the Two Opinions

On these suppositions the two opinions proposed at the Council of Trent must be combined to form a single principle: The episcopal power is sacramentally conferred; as the power of Christ it makes up a single and complete entity, namely, the power of both orders and jurisdiction. This sacramentally conferred power is ordered to this end: that it be exercised in the Church as an external society. For the salvific work of Christ our Lord which is to be continued to the end of time is in the hands of the Church. Exercise of episcopal power that is independent or not incorporated within the Church, the hierarchical society, is unlawful.

Therefore we must stress this distinction in regard to the bishop's power of governing: 1) *The substance of the power of jurisdiction, which is the spiritual, intentional being itself,* inherent in the sacramental episcopal character. This is constituted by the relationship (appointment) of the consecrated bishop to government in the Church, but lacks all concrete determination with regard to subjects. 2) The external *"form"* of the power of jurisdiction possessed through incorporation of the consecrated bishop within the Church, the external and hierarchical society, in virtue of the power of governing that has been sacramentally conferred upon him in its substance. Such incorporation is effected through the *canonical mission* (Can. 109). When this *essential* element of form is lacking, the power of governing is not completely constituted because it lacks its requisite external structure (in the Church) so that it cannot be efficaciously exercised. Only with the canonical mission is the power of governing that was substantially conferred in episcopal consecration rendered efficacious (i.e., *the efficacious or valid exercise of this power is given*). The consecrated bishop acquires his position in the hierarchy of jurisdiction; thus the concrete exercise of his power is coordinated with the power of the rest of the bishops.

Therefore, the two elements that are required by divine law in the efficacious power of jurisdiction are so related that the divine origin of the power, namely, the sacramental conferral, is coupled with a necessary coordination in its exercise with the power of the rest of the bishops, as well as with its dependence upon the primatial power. Actually this is the foundation for the explanation of the entire historical development of the creation of a bishop. Invariably the episcopal power in its substance, which constitutes a totality containing the powers of orders and jurisdiction, always has been, always is, and always will be given in episcopal consecration. This power is ordered to the Church. The exercise of this power when not incorporated within the Church is unlawful and indeed, in the case of the power of jurisdiction, invalid or juridically inefficacious[3] because the exercise of the power of jurisdiction of its very nature directly affects social life.

In antiquity such incorporation was had through lawful episcopal consecration (namely, approved by the co-provincial bishops and the Metropolitan) for a determined particular Church (diocese); then from the High Middle

127

Ages (under the Law of Decretals) through the Metropolitan's confirmation of the candidate who had been canonically elected by the cathedral chapter; finally, through canonical institution on the part of the Roman Pontiff. But all of these methods of incorporation contain the formality of the canonical mission since they confer a particular position in the hierarchy of the Church. Accordingly, the canonical mission is required by divine law for the valid exercise of the power of jurisdiction. But the concrete method of conferring the canonical mission is subject to human law (as determined by the Church's supreme governing power) and is consequently subject to historical development.

CONCLUSION

The two opinions advanced in the Council of Trent are combined by this explanation to form a *genuine synthesis*. The view supporting the conferral of episcopal power in episcopal consecration is combined with the view supporting the dependence of the efficacious (valid) power of governing upon the primatial power. Accordingly, this latter view, which has been perhaps more common, but never the comon view after the Council of Trent because of an unawareness of the historical development, is not relinquished but retained because it affirms the dependence of the efficacious power of governing upon the primatial power. For we must stress that the documents of the Pontiffs and the texts of authors who derive the power of jurisdiction from the Roman Pontiff certainly understand an *efficacious* power. Furthermore, the canonical mission must truly be said to be the cause of the efficacious power of governing in the Church under this aspect, because it brings about the relationship of the superiority of the bishop to his subjects in the concrete order.

Truly, the episcopal office of "tending the flock of God" (1 Pet. 5:2) or of "ruling the Church of God" (Acts 30:28) was instituted by Christ our Lord and is to be sacramentally conferred in order that it may be exercised in the Church which has been entrusted to the Roman Pontiff—to whom alone are addressed the words "I shall give you the keys of the Kingdom of Heaven" (Mt. 16:19)—in union with him "for the building up of the body of Christ . . . which is the Church . . . in love" (Eph. 4:16; Col. 1:24). Since the bishops' power of jurisdiction cannot be efficaciously exercised independently of the Roman Pontiff, the unity of the government of the Church is preserved by the primatial power of the Roman Pontiff as the Vicar of Christ. Hence true communion and the love of Christ are constantly established and perfected anew among the particular churches by the primatial power.

1. Divine Law, Human Law, and the Bishops' Power of Jurisdiction

Personal government

According to the preceding exposition the bishops' power of governing is simultaneously of divine and human law. The episcopal office is of *divine* law because the gift of the Holy Ghost and the conferral of the power of governing in its substance are had in episcopal consecration for the purpose of governing in the Church. (Of course, there is also the conferral of the power of orders, but we can prescind from this in the present context.) The epis-

129

copal office is of *human* law because the subjects in the concrete order as well as the concrete causes that are subject to the consecrated bishops' power of governing are determined by the canonical mission. For this reason (the canonical mission, by which the passive subject is determined by human law as established by the supreme governing power in the Church) the passive subject of the episcopal office can be increased or diminished. Consequently historical development and change (e.g., of diocesan boundaries) can and do occur. Also historical development is responsible for some "division" of episcopal faculties for ruling in the Church because there are bishops to whom other bishops and their dioceses are subject, namely, the Metropolitans, Primates, and Patriarchs. And there is also the case of the establishment of "a particular Church" to be governed by a bishop which has no territorial boundaries, but is established for the faithful of another rite in Latin territory or for the faithful in military service, etc.

Although, therefore, the canonical mission is required by divine law for any efficacious (valid) exercise of the episcopal power of governing, the possession of a concrete, canonical mission by a bishop, Metropolitan, Primate or Patriarch is of human law. For the sacramentally conferred power of governing is undetermined with regard to its passive subject. Although it is certainly a power ordered to the possession of government in the Church, nonetheless divine law requires that the exercise of this power be coordinated with the exercise of the power of the rest of the bishops. But this coordination (at the same time a restriction upon the exercise of the power, because no bishop possesses personal government throughout the entire Church except the Roman Pontiff to whom God

Himself has entrusted the government of the entire Church) is of human law. Consequently human law is responsible for the recognition and specification of the power of governing which the bishop can efficaciously exercise so that, if this recognition and specification are lacking, the efficacious exercise of the power of governing is not possessed.

Hence it is clear that the limits of the efficacious exercise of the power of the episcopal office are of human law. The ordinary power of jurisdiction is constituted by the faculties that are connected with the office by human law (although the power, exercised in virtue of these faculties, is of divine law in the sense in which this was explained above). Such faculties can be said to be based upon divine law to the degree that they are necessary for the ordinary government of the diocese under normal circumstances. It should be noted, however, that even such a faculty can and perhaps ought to be reserved to the Holy See in certain circumstances for the sake of the common good of the Church. For the coordination of the exercise of the power of governing of all the bishops includes specific subjection to the primatial power. Furthermore, the bishops can possess faculties by human law that do not seem to be necessary for the ordinary government of the diocese under normal circumstances, but belong of themselves to the primatial power. Such faculties constitute delegations by the law.

Similarly the faculties which the Metropolitans, Primates, and Patriarchs have in accordance with law are determined by human law (as established of the supreme governing power in the Church). For this reason the faculties constitute each office as ordinary jurisdiction. And in this case, too, faculties can be added which, while

131

firmly established, are nonetheless given as delegations by law because of themselves they belong to the primatial power.

Conclusion: The episcopal power of governing in the Church is of divine law, namely, the power of Christ sacramentally conferred. The efficacy of this power, the limits within which this power can be efficaciously exercised, is of human law. And this principle explains the entire historical development of the efficacious ordinary power of bishops, Metropolitans, Primates and Patriarchs without placing an artificial interpretation, i.e., one that does not harmonize with historical reality, upon the historical facts themselves.[4]

Collegiate Government

Collegiate exercise, or the exercise by several bishops together or acting as one body, of the power of jurisdiction must be explained in the same way. The power collegiately exercised is the power of Christ our Lord that is sacramentally conferred in its substance. It must, however, be determined by a canonical mission by which it can be efficaciously and collegiately exercised in the concrete order. Actually, in accordance with the norm of current legislation, the collegiate exercise of the power of governing is had—we are prescinding from an Ecumenical Council— in a particular council, namely, provincial and plenary councils. Titular bishops, who do not possess the government of a diocese, have a deliberative voice in the councils in which they lawfully participate.

Conclusion: The following can be said about the bishops' collegiate government. The power itself of governing, to be exercised collegiately, is derived from divine

possesses all of the power which the Lord has transmitted to the Church. The bishops, either individually or collectively as a body, have no efficacious power to govern independently of the Roman Pontiff, because on this supposition the Roman Pontiff would no longer be the Vicar of Christ to whom has been entrusted all the power of Christ the Lord, which He has transmitted to the Church. *The body of bishops with the Roman Pontiff* has the same power, but it can be exercised only to the extent to which the Roman Pontiff grants the faculty for the collegiate handling of an issue.

Hence the Roman Pontiff in the exercise of his plenary power represents Christ our Lord as His Vicar. The body of bishops in the exercise of the plenary power together with the Roman Pontiff represent Christ our Lord collegiately. Consequently the power itself in either case is not different; for it is always the power of Christ our Lord, which He has transmitted to the Church and which is to be exercised as the supreme power of the Church. And there is no difference either in the juridical value of juridical acts (everything else being equal) or in the obligation which they impose upon subjects.

But there is a difference in the way of representing the authority and power of Christ our Lord: The Roman Pontiff when acting alone represents more the unicity of the power of Christ our Lord over the entire Church since He is the unique Mediator in the New Testament between God and man. The body of bishops when acting together with the Roman Pontiff represents more the universality of the authority and power of Christ our Lord since His power extends to all nations, territories, and times. Hence the collegiate act, although it has no greater juridical value and imposes no greater obligation on subjects (everything else being equal) than the personal act of the Roman Pontiff, contains the formality of more extensive representation.[5] This representation is of great social significance because the suitable representation of social authority in the exercise of public power always has special significance among all people. Thus, for example, certain public acts are customarily performed with greater or the utmost public solemnity. Furthermore, the collegiate act of the body of bishops joined with the Roman Pontiff can in fact have more efficacy because such collegiate action is sometimes more readily accepted, since in such an act the communion of the bishops among themselves and with the Roman Pontiff, namely, the communion of the entire Church, is visibly and externally apparent. Finally, there is no doubt that the Roman Pontiff can lawfully revoke a law established for the entire Church by an Ecumenical Council under the same necessary suppositions that apply to the revocation of any law enacted by himself or his predecessors. But as a matter of fact such a law enjoys greater stability because of the greater solemnity which accompanied its enactment, namely, the cooperation of the entire body of bishops.

Consequently, whether it is a question of an act of the supreme power posited by the Roman Pontiff along with the body of bishops (Mt. 18:18) or a question of an act of the supreme power personally posited by the Roman Pontiff (Mt. 16:19), in either case we are concerned with the exercise of the power of Christ our Lord by the Church as the exercise of its supreme power. This power is immediately conferred upon both the Roman Pontiff and the bishops by Christ our Lord (in episcopal consecration). But the way in which this power is made efficacious differs. It becomes efficacious in the Roman

135

Pontiff, as the power of the Vicar of Christ, by divine law, namely, with a canonical election and acceptance thereof. It becomes efficacious in the bishops by the canonical mission, namely, the faculty from the Roman Pontiff for the collegiate handling of an issue.

Hence, in the exercise of the supreme power on the part of the body of bishops in union with the Roman Pontiff, the element that efficaciously constituted the supreme power is not exclusively the power of the Roman Pontiff but the power proper to the bishops[6] also, that power which is immediately conferred by Christ our Lord, even if it cannot become efficacious independently of or separate from the Roman Pontiff. It is true that the Roman Pontiff can accomplish the same juridical effect by his mere personal activity. For example, if the Roman Pontiff promulgates an Apostolic Constitution in an Ecumenical Council, the entire Church is held to its observance. Nevertheless, this does not involve an act of the Council itself, a collegiate act, unless there was at least a discussion of the issue.

It should also be noted that the Roman Pontiff, even though engaged in personal activity, bears witness to the faith of the entire Church or testifies that the universal norm which he has personally enacted is in harmony with the mandates which Christ our Lord gave to the entire Church.[7] This is the reason why in the strict sense of this term the legislative power for the entire Church cannot be delegated in a general way to the Roman Curia by the Roman Pontiff: because it involves infallibility.[8]

Conclusion: There is present in the Church only one supreme power which is the power of Christ our Lord entrusted to the Church. This power is represented in two modes of activity: 1) through the Roman Pontiff

136

personally, since he is the Vicar of Christ; 2) through the body of bishops, if and insofar as it acts collegiately with the Roman Pontiff, the Head of the body of bishops. Since the Roman Pontiff is the Vicar of Christ, even the body of bishops is subject to him.

The supreme power of the Church considered in its substance and in its efficacious exercise in the Roman Pontiff is derived from divine law. The supreme power of the body of bishops considered in its substance and in the necessity of having faculties from the Roman Pontiff for any efficacious exercise, impossible without the Roman Pontiff, is derived from divine law. Considered in its concrete efficacious exercise, this is derived from human law, namely it derives from the law by which the Roman Pontiff decides the causes which it can handle, its procedure, etc.

Accordingly, in the light of the supreme power of the Church the two views on the origin of the bishops' power of jurisdiction are also reduced to a common principle which constitutes a true synthesis of both opinions: the power itself is derived from divine law since the collegiate exercise of the power of governing is the power of Christ the Lord and is sacramentally conferred by Him; but the determination of causes in the concrete which are collegiately handled, as well as the determination of the way in which this collegiate exercise is to be organized, are derived from human law.

This principle explains the complete historical development of the Ecumenical Councils, at least regarding this point: the concrete manner in which the Roman Pontiff participates in an Ecumenical Council and exercises his function as Head is derived from human law and therefore is subject to historical development.

2. THE COLLEGIATE EXERCISE OF THE SUPREME POWER ON THE PART OF THE BODY OF BISHOPS TOGETHER WITH THE ROMAN PONTIFF

Concerning the question of why the body of bishops can collegiately exercise the supreme power along with the Roman Pontiff, the only possible reply is that the Roman Pontiff as the Vicar of Christ has the power to decide what kind of causes are to be thus treated, as well as the time, place and procedure. The Pontiff is not bound and cannot be obliged juridically in this regard;[9] for, if we suppose otherwise, he would no longer be the Vicar of Christ. But the nature of the issue and the condition of the Church can be such that the solution of a question through the collegiate exercise of supreme power on the part of the body of bishops together with the Roman Pontiff would be more or less opportunely applied because of the de facto greater efficacy of such a collegiate action. In this matter the Church entrusts herself to divine providence which firmly, graciously, and efficaciously arranges what is necessary for the Church. Actually, these principles are the basis of the juridical norms that govern an Ecumenical Council which is to be considered an extraordinary exercise of the supreme power.

There are also other ways to exercise the supreme power collegiately. For example, the ordinary magisterium which all bishops in their own diocese share with regard to certain revealed truths together with the Roman Pontiff is considered as an exercise of the supreme power. We are prescinding in the present context from these ways in which the body of bishops together with the Roman Pontiff can act more or less collegiately. But the moot question at present, on the occasion of the Second Vatican

138

Council, concerns the participation of the body of bishops in the ordinary government of the universal Church.

In accordance with previously explained principles it seems that the following comments must be made on this question: *The dogmatico-juridical necessity* for the participation of the body of bishops in the Roman Pontiff's ordinary government over the universal Church cannot be affirmed. For on the one hand, the power of such government is present in its entirety in the Roman Pontiff himself, and on the other hand, granted such a necessity, the Roman Pontiff would no longer be the Vicar of Christ because he would not have the full power of Christ our Lord entrusted to the Church. Truly, Christ our Lord put no restrictions upon the Supreme Pontiff's vicariate. Further still, such a restriction was excluded by the First Vatican Council since it taught that the Roman Pontiff has immediate episcopal power over all bishops and over all the faithful.

In consideration of the function of greater social representation and the actually greater efficacy of the activity of the body of bishops along with the Roman Pontiff, reasons can be advanced from the social order to render such participation of the body of bishops in the ordinary government of the universal Church fitting and *opportune*. On the other hand we must take into consideration the *difficulties* that such participation can occasion for the Church's good because under ordinary circumstances the collegiate act is a difficult undertaking. The greater the number of people participating in the activity of government, the greater the difficulty of acquiring unanimity of opinion. But prompt and firm action is especially demanded of the executive office of any public power. Accordingly no *general norm* can be established here except the following: in consideration of all the historical and social circumstances of the entire Church, that participation of the body of bishops in the ordinary government of the universal Church is fitting and opportune, which is more profitable for the common good of the Church.

It should be noted, however, that this decision on the convenience, amount, and method of such participation of the body of bishops in the ordinary government of the universal Church is ultimately up to the discretion of the Roman Pontiff who can, of course, opportunely deliberate on the question even by means of an Ecumenical Council. Actually our reigning Pontiff, Paul VI, in an Allocution to the Roman Curia on September 21, 1963, manifested his mind on this subject in these words:

> And we shall say further: when the Ecumenical Council manifested the desire to see some representatives of the episcopacy, particularly from among the prelates who direct a diocese, associated in a certain way and for certain questions, in accordance with the teaching of the Church and with canon law, with the supreme Head of the same Church in the care and responsibility of ecclesiastical government, the Roman Curia will surely not be in opposition since it will rather consider that the honor and burden of its sublime and indispensable service are increased because, apart from the due process of the ecclesiastical tribunals, whether in the Roman Curia or in the diocese, it is specifically administrative, consultive, and executive as we well know.[10]

Of course nothing is established relative to the concrete manner and really not even to the very fact of such participation of the body of bishops in the ordinary government of the universal Church. And it is not our purpose to treat these concrete questions in these pages. We would only wish to note that, in consideration of the Supreme Pontiff's manifestation of his mind, cited above, it cannot be said on this subject that the Ecumenical Council does not have the faculty to treat this subject. For there is no cause in the Church which is not subject to the supreme power of the Church, namely, to the Roman Pontiff even if he is acting in union with the Fathers of an Ecumenical Council. The Roman Curia is, of course, an instrument of the Roman Pontiff as the Vicar of Christ. And the opinion that the Roman Pontiff is the Vicar of Christ because he is the Head of the body of bishops is also justly denied.[11] Nevertheless the office of the Vicar of Christ, since it is of divine institution, constitutes a single authoritative whole. This authoritative whole is composed of several faculties which can indeed be distinguished, but not separated, from one another. Hence there cannot be any matter in the Church which is indeed subject to the Roman Pontiff, the Vicar of Christ, but is not subject to the Roman Pontiff when acting together with the bishops, namely, the Roman Pontiff acting as the Head of the body of bishops together with the bishops. In reality the body of bishops together with the Roman Pontiff is constituted by divine law, the primordial subject of supreme power in the Church, to which is subordinated every subject of power that exists in the Church by human law.

Finally, it seems that we should note—because it might be a question of representatives of the body of bishops, not the body of bishops itself—that a consultative function would be fitting for such a representative body in virtue of which a true, direct influence would be had on the government of the universal Church. Furthermore, the Roman Curia should have representatives in the representative body. For while the other representatives, although intent upon the common good of the Church in such consultation, almost necessarily take into considera-

141

tion, and indeed justly so, the circumstances in their own church or territory, there should be proper representation of that organ in the Church which of its very nature would directly take into consideration in such consultation the common good of the universal Church, and which would be able to afford information in this regard that would scarcely be forthcoming otherwise.

3. CONCLUSIONS ON THE COLLEGIALITY OF THE BODY OF BISHOPS

1. The bishops do not constitute a college in virtue of episcopal consecration considered in itself alone. Nevertheless, episcopal consecration does constitute the *sacramental foundation* of the collegiality of the bishops inasmuch as it confers the episcopal office; that is to say, the episcopal power which inheres in the character of the episcopal order is given with the gift of the Holy Ghost. This power also includes the power of governing which is ordered to this end: that it be exercised in the Church, the hierarchical society entrusted to the Roman Pontiff as the Vicar of Christ. In virtue of episcopal consecration the bishops fundamentally constitute a unit because they all participate in a specific way in the priesthood of Christ, the high priest of the New Testament, by means of the sacramental episcopal character.[12]

Formally, however, the bishops are constituted a college by the consecrated bishops' acquisition through a canonical mission of the efficacy of the power of governing, that was substantially conferred in episcopal consecration—in accordance with the norms of law as established by the Church's supreme governing power, which is non-existent without the Roman Pontiff. For this power must be exercised as a power coordinated with the power of all the bishops and, in particular, with the primatial power of the Roman Pontiff; in other words, this power must be exercised as the instrument of the Holy Ghost in the Church which has been hierarchically established under the Roman Pontiff as the Vicar of Christ. (Accordingly, the incorporation of a consecrated bishop within the college of bishops is formally accomplished by the canonical mission. We are prescinding from the question of whether a consecrated bishop acquires the juridically efficacious exercise of the power of governing because he is incorporated into the college of bishops, or whether the consecrated bishop is incorporated into the college of bishops because he acquires the exercise of the power of jurisdiction.)

Moreover, this power of governing which has been made efficacious by the canonical mission can be exercised not only personally, but also on the part of all the bishops together with the Roman Pontiff, although the establishment of this latter efficacy in the concrete is left to the discretion of the Roman Pontiff.

2. The collegiality of the body of bishops, considered as the exercise of the power of governing by all of them together, is, therefore, derived from *divine law* because the power exercised by the body of bishops together with the Roman Pontiff is in each and every bishop the power constituted by Christ our Lord and immediately, sacramentally conferred by Him (in episcopal consecration). Moreover, the dependence of the exercise of this power upon the Roman Pontiff is also derived from divine law. This collegiality is derived from *human law* since the

determination in the concrete of the causes to be treated and the way of treating them is left to the discretion of the Roman Pontiff.

3. Even in the case of the collegiality of the body of bishops the two views on the origin of the bishops' power of jurisdiction are reduced to a common principle which constitutes a true synthesis of both opinions. The power which is exercised—whether personally through a bishop who is incorporated in the college of bishops or by all the bishops in a body together—is in its substance derived from divine law since this power is the power of Christ our Lord which has been entrusted to the Church and sacramentally conferred upon each bishop. Moreover, the necessity of having a canonical mission for any efficacious exercise of this power, whether personal or through all together, is also derived from divine law. The constitution of the efficacy of this power in the concrete is derived from human law since the determination of the causes to be handled by all of them together and the way of handling them is left to the discretion of the Roman Pontiff, the Vicar of Christ. This consideration also makes clearer the essential function which the primatial office has in the constitution of collegiality in its exercise and thus in the preservation of unity of government in the Church.

4. Collegiality, constituted as explained above, has been present in the Church since the very beginning, although the concrete way in which incorporation into the college of bishops occurs and in which the constitution of the efficacy of the exercise of the power of governing by all the bishops together is had, is subject to historical development because it is of human law.

And the designation of the body of bishops as a college,

although the practice for centuries now, was not always in use. In the first centuries usage centered more around "*the communion*" of the particular churches which was had by "the communion" of their bishops and constituted by a *sacramental and juridical bond*. The bishops did not govern their own Churches (dioceses) as individuals without any relationship to the rest of the bishops, but as individuals joined by the sacramental-juridical bond which preserves and vivifies the "one holy Church" or the union of all the churches in the love of Christ.[13] From the very beginning special importance was assigned to the Church of Rome and hence to its Bishop in this "communion." Whoever was in "communion" with him, was in "communion" with the entire Church. The bishops, therefore, in virtue of the exercise of the power of governing in the Church by means of the canonical mission proper to each of them (the subjects and causes, as bishops, Metropolitan, Primate, and Patriarch) constitute an organically composed body under the Roman Pontiff as its head. This body constitutes a college since it can act collegiately in accordance with the norms of law. Moreover, even the exercise of the power of ruling by the individual bishops constitutes an exercise of the same power of Christ which is subject in everything to the same norms of divine and human law.

5. *The structure of the college of bishops is completely distinctive* and cannot be compared with the structure of other colleges, not even of the colleges which are found in the Church. The structure of the college of bishops is revealed in the theological, historical, and canonical data on the personal and joint exercise of the episcopal office. Actually in the question of the collegiality of the episcopacy we are also dealing with the *mystery of the Church* since the bishops in virtue of the sacramental episcopal character

are united with Christ the Lord. Hence in Him they are united by charity with one another and with the Roman Pontiff to promote the good of the Church by the exercise of the power of Christ which was conferred upon them to bring about and protect the life of Christ in the faithful.

Notes

1. "Episcopacy, presbyterate, and diaconate appear in the ancient documents less as a ritual function than as a charism destined for the building up of the Church. But it is worth noting that these charisms are not purely individual. They form orders which in their hierarchy are like the very structure of the Church and ought to assure its growth and the sanctification of its members" (B. Botte, O.S.B., "L'ordre d'après les prières d'ordination," Études sur le sacrement de l'ordre [Paris: Du Cerf, 1957], p. 34). "A theology of the priesthood should take as its point of departure the ordo episcoporum as the principle of the apostolicity and unity of the Church, not only in the sense of a narrow juridicism which would see in it only an external discipline, but in the theological sense of the word. It is due to a charism which is transmitted by the imposition of hands that the bishops with the assistance of the presbyterate have built up the Church. The Church ought to grow further still by means of them" (B. Botte, O.S.B., "Caractère collégial du presbytérat et de l'Episcopat," ibid., p. 123).

2. Even after the Council of Trent the opinion defending the conferral of the power of jurisdiction in episcopal consecration was constantly proposed, and sometimes restricted—under the influence of the Tridentine discussions and thus also because of ignorance of the historical development—to the bishops' collegiate exercise of the universal power of jurisdiction. Although there were many problems under this heading which were incapable of a ready speculative solution, it should be indicated nonetheless that this opinion was justly represented as the continuation of a very ancient tradition. Actually it was recognized as such by the Holy See on the occasion of the preparation for the First Vatican Council when a solution had to be presented to the question of the right of titular bishops to participate in the Council.

In the ninth meeting of the directive Congregation on May 17, 1868, Monsignor Angelini, the recorder, among other proposals made the following: "The reasoning behind the opposite opinion is based completely upon the assertion that the right to vote, or to have a voice in a council belongs to the power of jurisdiction. Now the simply titular bishops have no effective and actual jurisdiction. Hence they conclude that they lack the basis on which the right to vote rests.

"Yet this total lack of jurisdiction does not seem admissible since it is almost impossible not to acknowledge that at least some jurisdiction was received through the imposition of hands or consecration. Therefore, it is necessary to distinguish in a bishop the particular jurisdiction for the governing of some determined Church, which is inevitably received from the Pope, from the general and universal jurisdiction which the bishop acquires in the act of, and in virtue of his ordination, i.e., when he becomes a member of the episcopal body. . . . Such is the reasoning of Bolgeni, Cappellari who was afterwards Gregory XVI of holy memory, Phillips, and others.

"Moreover, it does not seem at all necessary to pass over in silence what not a few eminent authors remark on the subject of this same particular jurisdiction of the titular Bishops in relation to their respective churches: that, although these bishops are prevented from undertaking the government of these churches, there always remains with them a jurisdiction which is radical, habitual and, as they say, *in actu primo* and that its exercise remains suspended only *per accidens* and *in actu secundo*. And on this point the above-cited Apostolic Letter of Benedict XIV to the Cardinal of Lanze can also be conferred in which it is shown that this habitual jurisdiction is somewhat more effective and real than is ordinarily believed."

In this same Congregation's meeting of March 14, 1869, the following is stated: that when the reply distinguishing habitual from actual jurisdiction is left out by otherwise eminent and serious authors in response to the objection usually advanced in opposition and drawn from the fact that titular bishops lack jurisdiction, there is another solid distinction between the particular jurisdiction over a given diocese, which the titular bishops cannot exercise and the general and universal jurisdiction acquired in virtue of the same ordination and common to all bishops. This jurisdiction consists precisely in the right to teach and to govern the entire Church. . . . In view of all these weighty considerations, the mentioned most eminent and most reverend Cardinals have unanimously concluded that they do not see any way to deny admission to the Council even to a part of the above-mentioned titular bishops" (Mansi, "*Sacrorum Conciliorum nova et amplissima collectio*, 49 [1923], col. 495 f. 525 f.).

Hence it is clear that—just as with the authors who since the second half of the last century practically follow Bouix in this matter—the qualification of the view that defended the conferral of the power of jurisdiction in episcopal consecration as a singular view which was proposed almost exclusively by Bolgeni has no foundation. Rather there is a constant tradition on this subject and a genuinely Roman one since these authors, who affirm the conferral of the power of jurisdiction in episcopal consecration assert and faithfully defend, no less strongly than the others, the primatial rights of the Roman Pontiff. (It should be noted that one of the Fathers brought out this fact in the discussions on the episcopacy in the second session of the Second Vatican Council.)

3. "There were some, alas, there were some who, fearing the worldly

commands of men more than the sacrosanct judgments of God, give in to the orders of the persecutors, going so far as to receive sacrilegious episcopal consecration from which surely no jurisdiction can arise since is was performed without an 'Apostolic mandate' " (John XXIII, in a secret consistory, AAS 50 [1958], 983). This passage refers to schismatic episcopal consecration in China. For this reason it has no recognition in the Church: it lacks canonical form so that of itself efficacious jurisdiction could not be had. "As a matter of fact, through consecration a bishop receives both the power of orders and the power of jurisdiction so that he is apt for the administration of grace and for the government of the Church in dependence upon Peter the Head. . . . For the bishop furnished with this twofold power by consecration should not be considered as it were atomically or individually, but as ordered to the structure and life of the Mystical Body and included therein. . . . But the power of jurisdiction can also be impeded as regards the validity of its exercise. For, although it is rooted in the consecrated bishop, according to current legislation it can in no way burst into exercise without the approval of the Roman Pontiff" (Carolus Molari, "Adnotationes de natura potestatis hierarchicae Ecclesiae," *Divinitas*, 6 [1962] 571 f.).

4. Consequently the two opinions on the nature of the office of the (Oriental) Patriarch also seem capable of reduction to a single principle. Doubtless this office with its constitutive faculties owes its origin to historical development. Hence such faculties are derived from human law as established by the supreme governing power of the Church, even though perhaps the result of custom. Therefore, this office is based upon a very ancient title of law, namely, a supremely venerable tradition which the supreme authority of the Church hardly ever touches. Nevertheless, from the very nature of the thing this office as ecclesiastical is subject to this authority and its constitutive faculties depend upon it, even though the power to be so exercised is conferred—*quoad substantiam*—in episcopal consecration.

5. "For since the bishops, when summoned by the Supreme Pontiff to share responsibility, are not mere counsellors but, as true judges and decision-makers, publish decrees along with the Pope, and since these decrees are certainly supremely authoritative and bind the entire Church, there can be no doubt that the bishops have some share in the teaching and governing of the entire Church. But since it is no less certain and has been defined by the canon of the third chapter in the first constitution on the Church that the Roman Pontiff does not possess merely a more important part but rather the plenitude of supreme power, it follows that this power is present in two subjects, in the body of bishops joined to the Pope and in the Pope alone. And this may seem difficult. Yet it is not new; it was commonly admitted by those also who were defending the side of the Roman Pontiff in the controversy which arose after the Councils of Constance and Basel. The testimony of Bellarmine should be sufficient in this regard. He says: 'The same men who teach that the

Pope is above a council which is held without him teach that there is intensively equal authority in the Pope alone and in a council together with the Pope, granted that the power is extensively greater in the council: and consequently the Pope cannot be judged or condemned by such a council . . . because an equal does not have power over an equal' " (Joseph Kleutgen's report on the reformed schema in the First Vatican Council; Mansi, *Sacrorum Conciliorum nova et amplissima collectio,* 53 [1927], col. 321.

6. Confer the text of Fr. Kleutgen cited in the preceding note, "The subject of infallibility . . . is both the visible head of the Church considered in himself and this same visible head as composing and informing the body of the teaching Church, which is itself thus made (body with the head) infallible through the assistance of the Spirit of truth. The Vatican definition, which was described just a little while ago, indicates this inadequate distinction in the subject of infallibility. For in it the infallibility of the Pontiff in making an ex *cathedra* definition is compared with the infallibility of the Church when making a definition. The former is directly and purposely publicly proclaimed by the Council; the latter is supposed as certain and assumed as a term of comparison" (John Baptist Franzelin, S.J., *Tractatus de divina Traditione et Scriptura,* [Romae, 1896⁴], pp. 109 f.). Can 1323 § 2, also seems to intimate a twofold subject of the supreme power.

The opinion explained in the text above seems to harmonize well with the acts of our happily reigning Supreme Pontiff Paul VI, although of course the question as such is not formally proposed therein: a) For the formula with which the Supreme Pontiff approved the decrees at the end of the second session of the Second Vatican Council (December 4, 1963) reads as follows: "In the Name of the Most Holy and Undivided Trinity, Father, Son and Holy Ghost. The decrees, which were just read in this Sacrosanct and Universal Second Vatican Synod which has been lawfully assembled, were acceptable to the Fathers." . . . "And We, by the Apostolic power transmitted to Us by Christ, approve decree and establish in the Holy Ghost these decrees along with the Venerable Fathers, and command that what was thus established in the synod to the glory of God be promulgated." b) In an Allocution to the Roman Curia on December 24, 1963, the following is found: "See to it that the Council is helped by your ready industry to attain quickly the conclusions which enjoy the supreme support of the Pope in union with that of the assembly of the Conciliar Fathers. The holding of the Council is not (as a certain uninformed and imprudent newsman has suggested) a show of force between opposing powers, but is rather the expression of one and the same supreme power which is uttered with one single voice, that proceeds from that of the Conciliar Members joined with the sovereign voice of the Pope; and that is a moment of supreme communion of minds and judgments when the Roman Church especially ought to do all in its power to arrange that the moment of the greatest manifestation of authority may coincide in aspect and in spirit with the moment of greatest charity" (*Osservatore Romano*, December 25, 1963, p. 3).

7. "Moreover, it must be noted that, if the body of bishops is not understood to be the bishops assembled in a Council but all of the bishops scattered throughout the world, it can never happen that in those things at least in which the Church cannot err or be lacking, the body of bishops, i.e., all or almost all of the bishops, would disagree with the Pope. . . . For just as the promise made to Peter would prove false if the Roman Pontiff should be in error when speaking *ex cathedra*, so would the promise made to the college of bishops prove false if the entire body of bishops should fall into error. . . . Therefore it is impossible for all of the bishops to go astray either from the truth in their teaching or from justice and holiness in their governing" (Joseph Kleutgen in the First Vatican Council, *op. cit.*, 332).

8. "Likewise, absolute legislative power, which is truly universal according to its supreme degree and in all matters, has in fact not been conceded and cannot lawfully be delegated to the Roman Congregations. For Suarez rightly comments (*De legibus* 1. IV, Cap. 6, n. 1.22): 'For certainly as far as absolute legislation is concerned through which a law receives its binding force over the entire Church without the special approval of the Roman Pontiff, such power does not seem to be able to be delegated or even committed to another. The reason for this is that canon laws which oblige the entire Church ought to proceed from a power which cannot err in matters pertaining to morals' " (Francis Xavier Wernz, S.J., *Ius Decretalium*, I [Romae, 1905²], 107.

9. "According to theologians the Pope is never obliged to have recourse to this exercise. . . . All theologians also agree in recognizing that there is never an absolute necessity to convoke a council or to have recourse to the exercise of collegiate power, although they stress all of the great advantages which it would obtain for the Church in certain circumstances" (F.-M.-R. Gagnebet, O.P., "La primauté pontificale et la collégialité de l'episcopat," *La France Catholique*, 885 [November 15, 1963], 6).

10. *AAS* 55 [1963], 799.

11. We are prescinding from this opinion in this context.

11. "But if each of the bishops is the sacred pastor of only the portion of the flock which has been entrusted to him, nevertheless, as a lawful successor of the Apostles, by divine institution and precept he is made responsible for the apostolic function of the Church along with the rest of the bishops in accordance with those words which Christ spoke to His Apostles: 'As the Father has sent Me, I also send you.' This mission which includes 'all nations even to the consummation of the world' did not in the least pass away when the Apostles passed from this mortal life. On the contrary it still continues in the bishops who are in communion with the Vicar of Jesus Christ" (Pius XII, *Encyclical, Fidei donum, AAS* 49 [1957], 237). Appealing to these words F. M. R. Gagnebet, O.P., re-

marks: "Just as Saint Celestin has already remarked in his letter to the Council of Ephesus, the bishop insofar as he is a member of the college is obliged to do his share towards the evangelization of the world" (Op. cit., p. 7). Actually every lawfully consecrated bishop is responsible under this title for the common good of the Church, although a canonical mission must be added for the possession of a concrete office.

13. Confer L. Hertling, S.J., "Communio und Primat," Miscellanea Historiae Pontificiae, VII [Rome, 1943], 43 f.—"This consciousness (concerning the priesthood of the Church) has two roots: the conviction that it is apostolic and the conviction that it is one and catholic. It is apostolic because its bishops have transmitted from generation to generation, along with the deposit of tradition, a charism which comes to them from the Apostles and, in the final analysis, from Christ. It is one and catholic because its bishops are mutually interdependent and because the ordo episcoporum by its communion preserves the unity of the Church which is scattered throughout the world." "In summary, what we ascertain at the time of the great councils is only the confirmation of what we find in the preceding centuries. The Ecumenical Council is nothing else than the ordo episcoporum which unites in order to exercise by common consent the charge which it has to rule the Church of God" (B. Botte, O.S.B., op. cit., pp. 121, 117).

A NOTE ON THE TYPE

IN WHICH THIS BOOK WAS SET

This book has been set in Electra, a type face created in 1935 by W. A. Dwiggins, the well-known Boston artist. This type falls within the "modern" family of type styles, but was drawn to avoid the extreme contrast between "thick and thin" elements that marks most "modern" type faces. The design is not based upon any traditional model, and is not an attempt to revive or to reconstruct any historic type. Since its birth, Electra has met with success because of its easy-to-read quality. This book was composed and printed by the York Composition Company, Inc., of York, Pa., and bound by Moore and Company of Baltimore, Md. The design and typography of this book are by Howard N. King.